Autism Is Not a Disease

Autism Is Not a Disease

The Politics of Neurodiversity

Jodie Hare

VERSO

London • New York

First published by Verso 2024
© Jodie Hare 2024

1 3 5 7 9 10 8 6 4 2

Verso
UK: 6 Meard Street, London W1F 0EG
US: 388 Atlantic Avenue, Brooklyn, NY 11217
versobooks.com

Verso is the imprint of New Left Books

ISBN-13: 978-1-80429-153-5
ISBN-13: 978-1-80429-155-9 (US EBK)
ISBN-13: 978-1-80429-154-2 (UK EBK)

British Library Cataloguing in Publication Data
A catalogue record for this book is available from the British Library

Library of Congress Cataloging-in-Publication Data

Names: Hare, Jodie, author.
Title: Autism is not a disease : the politics of neurodiversity / Jodie
   Hare.
Description: London ; New York : Verso, 2024. | Includes bibliographical
   references.
Identifiers: LCCN 2024006029 (print) | LCCN 2024006030 (ebook) | ISBN
   9781804291535 (paperback) | ISBN 9781804291559 (ebook)
Subjects: LCSH: Autism. | Neurodiversity--Political aspects.
Classification: LCC RC553.A88 H362 2024 (print) | LCC RC553.A88 (ebook) |
   DDC 616.85/882--dc23/eng/20240213
LC record available at https://lccn.loc.gov/2024006029
LC ebook record available at https://lccn.loc.gov/2024006030

Typeset in Fournier MT by Hewer Text UK Ltd, Edinburgh
Printed and bound by CPI Group (UK) Ltd, Croydon CR0 4YY

CONTENTS

For Irene and Thomas

All those movements that clear space and mark our struggle to live free, live better, love more, to knit abundance, all that is the work of another realm that is not-here.

— Lola Olufemi, *Experiments in Imagining Otherwise*

Sometimes it hurts just to stand. Sometimes a person needs help because she needs it, not because her story is compelling or noble or strange enough to earn it, and sometimes you just do what you can. It doesn't make you any better, or any worse. It doesn't change you at all, except for the split second when you imagine that day when you will be the one who has to ask.

— Leslie Jamison, *Make It Scream, Make It Burn*

INTRODUCTION

In the summer of 2016, I spent a month in a psychiatric ward. Months after one of the most difficult experiences of my life, I had just scraped my way through my first year of university and my depression was at its worst. I felt out of sync with my peers, and I was struggling to understand what it was that made me feel like, no matter how hard I tried, I could not keep up with them, or why something as simple as socialising or curating friendships felt like dragging my feet through mud. I felt alienated from other people, and that something inherent to me meant I would never be good at being a person. I could not shake the relentless depression I felt, and I thought that I could lighten the burden of the people I loved by not existing anymore.

Thanks to the patience and kindness of my loved ones and a therapist, I did make it through that summer. My mental health problems persisted, and I continued to seek out books and articles in which others shared their stories of similar issues – hoping that others might be able to put into words what felt indefinable. One day, I stumbled across a piece by a young woman who had been diagnosed with the disorder some doctors had put in my reports over the years: emotionally unstable personality disorder, otherwise known as borderline personality disorder (BPD). My therapist and I had discussed the disorder – a highly stigmatised diagnosis often applied to those with complex trauma – before, and we believed that, while I identified with some of its specified symptoms, it did not capture the sum of my experiences well enough. The article's author wrote that she too had been given a BPD diagnosis, but felt it did not fit. After further therapy she had discovered that she had been misdiagnosed – she was, in fact, autistic.[1]

I can admit I was misinformed about autism at the time. I was aware of the variations in the support needs associated with it, and of its effects on socialising, but since every autistic person I had met at that point was a boy or man, the image I held of an autistic person was a white male – one likely to have no friends at all; somebody who might have edged closer to the profile of characters like the one played by Dustin Hoffman in *Rain Man*. All the autistic people I knew had been diagnosed early on in life, and it did not seem to me as if this could have been something people around me would have missed.

I spent some time researching autism before I discussed it with a doctor, reading lots of people's personal experiences on the subject, particularly those of young women, whose experiences I felt more often reflected mine. I came to learn that lots of research was being conducted into the way in which those with marginalised identities – because of gender, race, class, and so on – might be overlooked in autism circles because so many of the original case studies focused on young, white, middle-class boys.

Eventually I visited my GP and asked her what she thought, explaining that I had received a myriad of diagnoses over the years, but that doctors had never felt completely certain in diagnosing me as one thing or another. She referred me to the charity MENCAP, which put me through some initial assessments. After almost three years on the waiting list, I received an official diagnosis from the Maudsley Hospital in the summer of 2020 – four years after my stay in hospital.

By this time I had discovered an online community of autistic people. I was overwhelmed by the number of people whose lives looked a little like mine, and how many of my experiences no longer felt alienating or strange. I was not the only person who felt like I belonged on a different planet, or who found interactions with others profoundly confusing. My adolescence had been filled with instances of accidentally falling into conflict with people because I had misread a social cue or overstepped my place because I had misunderstood social hierarchy. I repeatedly found that friendships I had invested in and thought were reciprocal were not as strong as I had thought, and that sometimes the people concerned simply tolerated me.

After years of so many embarrassing setbacks, by the time I started university my social anxiety was more of a hindrance than ever. After years of feeling as if I would never find somewhere I belonged, finally a small corner of the internet provided me with some comfort, as countless others shared stories of their vulnerability that matched my own.

Building up a vocabulary for my experience was empowering, but I was also saddened by the vast numbers of autistic people who had been through something traumatic or been regularly mistreated because the way they lived and understood the world was at odds with dominant norms. It made me angry – and the more I read, the angrier I became.

Other people were also angry, and continue to be. In many of the spaces I inhabited, people spoke about the concept of 'neurodiversity'. It was not just a palatable way of saying 'autistic' or 'disabled', which was how I had seen it used in commercial settings, but named a political movement filled with people who wanted to build a better world. I had already spent some years interested in feminist and queer theory. The more I learnt about the neurodiversity campaign, the clearer it became to me that the world it was seeking to create would benefit so many – beyond just those who understand themselves as neurodivergent.[2]

The neurodiversity campaign matters to me because I and other neurodivergent people I love have faced discrimination for approaching and understanding the world differently. Being neglected and mistreated in various settings has contributed to our wealth of mental health problems. My own stay in a psychiatric hospital exemplified a terrible statistic: that one in four autistic women are hospitalised for a psychiatric condition by the age of twenty-five.[3] The study that cites this figure, analysing data from people born in Sweden, indicates that this number is five times higher than for non-autistic women, and nearly twice as high as autistic men. This increased level of mental health problems affects the entire neurodivergent community, and is associated with higher rates of suicide.[4] For autistic people specifically, it predicts a life expectancy of just thirty-six years.[5]

As an increasing number of diagnoses are made and more people come to understand themselves as neurodivergent, we cannot just accept that huge numbers of people should live with such a low quality of life. It matters to me that neurodivergent people know they have as much of a right to a long, happy life as anyone else, and that they can feel this is reflected by the society in which they live.

This book provides an opportunity to explain to those new to the idea of neurodiversity why the campaign is an essential part of any broader fight for liberation. Forging a world where neurodivergent individuals are safe and supported requires the erasure of systemic injustices that also impact marginalised groups affected by discrimination based on disability, class, race, gender, sexuality, and more.

However, even as we gain a better understanding of it, the concept of neurodiversity is in the process of being watered down. The word is being stripped of its political potential. Neurodivergence is increasingly seen as a marketable attribute.

Companies are beginning to ask how they might use neurodivergent workers to increase profit margins. *Harvard Business Review* printed articles with titles like 'Neurodiversity Is a Competitive Advantage', concluding that 'the potential returns are great' and that managers should 'do the hard work of fitting irregular puzzle pieces together' (the 'irregular' pieces of course being the neurodivergent individuals themselves).[6]

Others believe that the term 'neurodiversity' is gaining traction because it is 'preferable to "disability" or words with a similarly negative connotation'.[7] This use of neurodiversity as a euphemism is rooted in ableism. It suggests that the word 'disability' should be avoided at all costs, that it is something to be ashamed of, or that there is something undesirable about attaching it to your personhood.

As well as failing to capture the aims of the campaign, this co-optation of 'neurodiversity' insinuates that those invested in the campaign are ashamed of the word 'disability' – which is also untrue.[8] As an autistic person who believes in the values at the heart of the neurodiversity campaign, this saddens me. Neurodiversity is one stepping stone along a road filled with opportunities for positive social change, and I do not want this political potential to be overlooked.

Many thinkers over the years have explained how societal systems are strengthened and maintained through the oppression of marginalised groups. Angela Davis, for instance, has explained that racism will not be eradicated without the concomitant eradication of racial capitalism, while others have discussed how homophobia cannot thrive without the workings of the patriarchy. Making changes to our society in the name of neurodiversity requires us to fix some of our wider issues with discrimination and poverty, while also thinking about access to health care, education, and much more.

Understanding neurodiversity as a political campaign inherently linked to every other cause for liberation means widening the net. It requires us to forge connections across various struggles and ask how solving one issue might offer a solution to others. As Marta Rose, a neurodivergent writer and artist, remarks on her Instagram: 'There is no liberation for neurodivergent people that doesn't float on a river moving all peoples and creatures towards freedom.'[9] This statement, as well as its inverse – that the liberation of all will not occur without liberation from neuronormativity – speaks to the core tenet of this book. The neurodiversity movement is an ever-growing part of a disability-informed battle for justice and equality.

I hope this book will contribute to our understanding of where neurodiversity fits alongside other social justice campaigns, and of how building this link between them will both strengthen the politics of the term and help offer answers for the question of what a better world for neurodivergent people, and thus everyone else, might look like. As David Graeber noted, 'The ultimate hidden truth of the world is that it is something that we make, and could just as easily make differently.'[10]

❧

A frequently misunderstood diagnosis, autism frames the neurodiversity campaign. It is the original subject of Judy Singer's 1998 thesis, 'Odd People In', where the term 'neurodiversity' was first used in an academic setting.[11] Written during the period in which access to the internet was becoming widespread and online chat rooms were becoming increasingly popular, Singer's thesis was the result of a growing community of autistic people talking to one another online.

While Singer is often now thought of as the 'godmother' of neurodiversity, a deeper look into the history of autistic communities shows that the word was born from shared discussions in spaces such as Martijn Dekker's Independent Living on the Autistic Spectrum (InLv) email list, and among activists like Jim Sinclair during the creation of Autism Network International. In these autistic-run spaces, connected for the first time by the internet, the growing neurodivergent community discussed their experiences and the value they thought could be found in neurological diversity.[12]

The sudden access among autistic people to other people who lived lives similar to their own led to a feeling of strength in numbers. The confirmation that there were others like them out there encouraged a sense that they had every right to live a valued life, despite whatever mainstream society might have to say on the matter.

Thanks to the size of the neurodiversity community and the number of competing ideas within it, there are, quite rightly, no clearly defined rules for who can now be considered neurodivergent, and many debates have been conducted about who should be included. While originally framed with autistic people in mind, neurodiversity is now thought to include:

- ADHD
- dyslexia
- dyscalculia
- dyspraxia
- learning disabilities
- acquired neurological conditions (such as traumatic brain injury)
- Down syndrome
- schizophrenia
- dementia
- Parkinson's disease
- long-term mental health conditions such as bipolar disorder

What makes these diagnoses significant is their ability to shape who a person is at their core. Unlike diagnoses of temporary or curable conditions, these affect the way a person interprets the world around them, how they process outside information and how they exist in the world. An often-cited quote from Jim Sinclair, one of the founding members of the Autism Network International, reads:

> Autism isn't something a person has, or a 'shell' that a person is trapped inside. There's no normal child hidden behind the

autism. Autism is a way of being. It is pervasive; it colors every experience, every sensation, perception, thought, emotion, and encounter, every aspect of existence. It is not possible to separate the autism from the person – and if it were possible, the person you'd have left would not be the same person you started with.[13]

As Singer eventually came to understand herself, as well as her mother and her daughter, as autistic, she engaged in online communities such as InLv, interviewing members and listening to their calls for a concept that represented them and provided new ways of looking at neurodivergence. It was after these crucial discussions that Singer took what she had learned into an academic setting. 'For me', she wrote, 'the significance of the "Autism Spectrum" lies in its call for and anticipation of a "Politics of Neurodiversity."'[14]

Singer has always emphasised that the movement was designed to be political, and that its intersection with other political categories renders it 'a paradigm for social change'.[15] Despite this politicisation, there are few analyses of the term's political potential, and there are few investigations into how it connects with other campaigns for liberation. This has led to an inevitable watering down of a term that was created to inspire radical political organising, a deconstruction of our understanding of 'normality', and a confrontation with the need for systemic change. This book aims to address this gap in understanding, making a direct argument for neurodiversity as a political campaign.

There are many components to the neurodiversity campaign, but I believe a good place to start is by highlighting how its inherent opposition to a pervasive medical pathologisation cements the depth of its political intent. This opposition rejects the idea that we should make value judgements about cognitive disabilities and use those judgements to determine whose lives are or are not worth living. It rejects the model that pathologises a disability as an individual issue, framing the disabled person's failure to meet a 'normal' standard as the central problem.

The campaign asks us to unpack our society's desire to define a 'normal' brain against one that functions differently. It demands that, instead of pathologising those who exist outside these predetermined norms, we recognise their existence as part of natural biological variation, as well as recognising our failure to support them, and begin to build a world in which they too can thrive. As disability justice organiser Mia Mingus says, we must begin

> moving away from an equality-based model of sameness and 'we are just like you' to a model of disability that embraces difference, confronts privilege and challenges what is considered 'normal' on every front. We don't want to simply join the ranks of the privileged; we want to dismantle those ranks and the systems that maintain them.[16]

I hope this book will encourage this process, prompting you as a reader not only to shift your understanding of neurodiversity and what must be done to support neurodivergent individuals, but also to confront the systems that continue to harm disabled people more widely, locating this harm along an axis of oppression that impacts all marginalised groups throughout society.

The book will walk you through the conception of the term 'neurodiversity', explaining the shifting nature of this term's definition. I will explain the ways it can be aligned with other social justice campaigns, and why we should not surrender its political character or accept its commodification. After explaining its connection to movements like Disability Justice, I will give a brief overview of work, life and material conditions for neurodivergent people and their families, before presenting some ideas on what we might look towards changing in the future – what working towards liberation might look like.

Much of the book will focus on autism and the experiences of autistic people, since this is what I know best. I hope my arguments will make it clear that they can and should be applied much more broadly, to incorporate the futures of all neurodivergent people. In a burgeoning movement, conversations around neurodiversity continue every day, with new ideas and practices being developed as I write these words. For this reason, it is highly possible – and indeed welcome – that much of what I write will become obsolete in both the immediate and more distant future.

1

THE NEURODIVERSITY
CAMPAIGN TODAY

In 1999, Judy Singer contributed to an academic series titled *Disability Discourse* published by the Open University. Her paper, titled '"Why Can't You Just Be Normal for Once In Your Life?" From a "Problem with No Name" to the Emergence of a New Category of Difference', detailed a burgeoning community of individuals who knew themselves to be different but lacked a name for what they described as 'hardwired neurological difference'. Frustrated with the lack of academic attention being paid to what she understood as the introduction of a new category of disability, she explained:

> The 'Neurologically Different' represent a new addition to the familiar political categories of class/gender/race and will augment the insights of the social model of disability. The rise of Neurodiversity takes postmodern fragmentation one step further. Just as the postmodern era sees every once too-solid belief melt into air, even our most taken-for-granted assumption – that we all more or less see, feel,

touch, hear, smell, and sort information, in more or less the
same way (unless visibly disabled) – are being dissolved.[1]

This term, popularised by Judy Singer but ultimately created
in autistic/neurodivergent communities, offered new perspectives on how human beings understand the world, giving shape
to the experiences of a group of individuals who were usually
written off as social outcasts and isolated for this difference.
They were, as Singer states, 'starting to fight back against the
exclusion and mistreatment – from ridicule to active bullying – that had been their lot'.[2] Singer believed that the three
categories that 'disability' was understood to include at that
time – physical, intellectual, psychiatric – did not properly
capture the experiences of 'high-functioning' autistic people
or those with Asperger syndrome (of which her work focused
and terms to which I will return shortly). For this reason, she
described them as 'disabilities in social communication'.

Neurodiversity is, at its core, a social movement tasked
with categorising something previously ignored while also
rejecting the disorder paradigm that perpetuates the idea of
a 'normal' brain and a 'non-normal' brain, ultimately serving
only to privilege those who are part of the 'normal' group. The
neurodiversity campaign does not accept that autistic people
and other neurodivergent people are inherently 'disordered'
compared to the rest of the population. It asserts that these
neurotypes are simply less common forms of neurocognitive
functioning, disabled by the hegemony and inaccessibility of
wider society.

While this may not superficially seem a radical idea, the discrimination that many neurodivergent individuals face proves otherwise. This discrimination is fuelled by ableism, entrenched in our societies in service of a status quo that marginalises and demonises those who deviate from the norm. I believe that it is also related to the context in which autism emerged as a disability.

Having been given many other names over the years, including 'childhood schizophrenia' and 'feeblemindedness', this disability acquired the name 'autism' within an ever-shifting political landscape. This haphazard history is a contributing factor to the whirlwind of ideas about what autism is, combined with shifts in the role of genetics and psychiatry, as well as growing political movements.

While most people attribute the term autism to the work of Austrian psychiatrist Leo Kanner following a paper he wrote in 1943, it was Eugen Bleuler who introduced the first seeds of the idea in 1911, while studying schizophrenia. He believed that autistic thinking was a method for avoiding 'unsatisfying realities', in which patients could turn away from reality by replacing it with fantasies and hallucinations. A few decades later, Kanner was the first to introduce the concept of autism to the world. His work made a larger distinction from the behaviour of children he believed could be classified as autistic as opposed to schizophrenic. This focus on childhood in the earliest research is notable not only as a reflection of Kanner's work on the world's first book on child psychiatry, but also as a reflection on autism research and understanding in the present day. Much of the research conducted continues to be around autistic children, neglecting the needs of autistic adults.

Working in Vienna at around the same time, in the 1940s, was Dr Hans Asperger. While his 1944 thesis was not widely known until Lorna Wing popularised it during the 1980s, it was his work that helped to expand the idea of an autism 'spectrum'. He was hailed for some years as a heroic figure in autism history, and the man behind the previously used term Asperger syndrome. But it has come to light in recent years that he was involved in the deaths of many disabled children under the Nazi regime. Describing autistic children as 'in opposition to Nazi Party values', Asperger is thought to have referred many sick or disabled children to the Am Spiegelgrund clinic in Vienna, where they were killed using barbiturates.[3]

So it seems that part of the history of autism emerged hand in hand with Nazi eugenics, with Asperger describing autistic children as outside 'the greater organism' of the Nazi ideal. This portrayal of autistic people as faulty is also likely to have led to discrimination before the concept of autism was even understood. In the UK, the Mental Deficiency Act of 1913 was created to treat 'moral defectives' – including those classified under the terms 'idiots', 'imbeciles', 'feeble-minded persons' and 'moral imbeciles'. This law was used to segregate groups of people from society, forcing many into asylums. It is thought that many of these individuals would today be described as having learning or developmental disabilities.[4] Given that many studies show that a large number of autistic people also have learning disabilities (although the numbers identified in these reports vary), it is not too much of a leap to suggest that some of these 'mental defectives' would have been autistic or otherwise neurodivergent.

We can see, therefore, that much of the earliest work on autism, neurodivergence and disability began from a position of prejudice and fear, asking how society could protect itself from those who were 'defective'. These grotesque attitudes are longstanding, and have contributed to the proliferation of ableist narratives, infiltrating cultures on a global scale and being partly responsible for the necessity of the neurodiversity campaign.

Among other factors, these early narratives have led to the pathologisation and subsequent isolation of autistic people from society. In order to combat this, Singer's earliest work frames neurodiversity using the social model of disability, as opposed to the medical model. She refuses to see autistic people as a burden to society, or as individuals who struggle to fit in because they are deficient in some way.

The medical model of disability is arguably the culturally more dominant of the two, and has been an underlying force behind the oppressive treatment of disabled people. It is defined as 'viewing disability as a problem of the person, directly caused by disease, trauma, or other health condition which therefore requires sustained medical care provided in the form of individual treatment by professionals'.[5] This model views the disabled person as the problem in need of a 'cure', unburdening institutions of the responsibility to build accessibility into their vision for the world – framing things like wheelchair ramps, braille signs and adequate seating as an afterthought or a desirable ideal, but not as essential.

With regard to neurodivergence, the medical model is inextricably linked to Nick Walker's description of the 'pathology paradigm' – a set of sociocultural assumptions with far-reaching consequences. As Walker writes,

> The pathology paradigm ultimately boils down to just two fundamental assumptions:
>
> 1. There is one 'right,' 'normal,' or 'healthy' way for human brains and human minds to be configured and to function (or one relatively narrow 'normal' range into which the configuration and functioning of human brains and minds ought to fall).
> 2. If your neurological configuration and functioning (and, as a result, your ways of thinking and behaving) diverge substantially from the dominant standard of 'normal,' then there is Something Wrong With You.[6]

Seeking to combat this narrative, many of those who believe in the neurodiversity campaign instead subscribe to the social model of disability. This sees disability as socially manufactured: something caused by a failure to integrate all individuals into society. Rather than an individual failing, disability is a complex matter informed by the social environment. For this reason, society is tasked with considering how best to manage disability, making modifications to ensure that no one is prevented from participating in social life. An example often given is that of a wheelchair user unable to access a building. The medical model suggests that the wheelchair user is the one with the issue, and that they should do everything they can to regain mobility. The social model, on the other hand, suggests that the answer is to install a ramp or other building modifications that will ensure accessibility.

This means that society's barriers, exclusionary practices and ableist narratives around disability are what shape a person's experience of disability. By using the social model of disability to inform her work, Singer rejects a stigmatised pathologisation of neurodivergence – what was previously understood as 'disease' becomes difference. But this is not a rejection of disability itself, as some suggest. Instead, she promotes the inclusion of disability through the lens of the social model.

This requires that we understand autism as a natural neuro-divergence, that autistic and other neurodivergent people have always existed, and that we will continue to exist. Autism is thus not a disease to be pathologised or 'cured', but a natural part of human existence that, while it brings its own challenges, is predominantly disabling because our social environments are constructed to isolate anyone who differs from a predetermined 'normal', which makes the lives of neurodivergent people much harder, preventing their access to and engagement with many parts of life, including education, socialising, sport, housing, health care, and much else.

Instead of framing us as outsiders who do not fit into society, the neurodiversity campaign understands that the way we have structured society does not successfully account for all its members. The movement is constructed around the idea that it is our job to rebuild society in a way that is accessible for every kind of life, and that we should seek to reduce the stigmatisation of those who have so often been shunned – including disabled people and those with severe mental health problems.

Expanding the Definition

When Singer first published her thesis in 1998, she centred her work around a very specific group of autistic people. She stated that she was referring only to those with 'high-functioning' autism, or Asperger syndrome, and those who were recorded as having 'normal' to 'high' intelligence. As many have since pointed out, this restrictive understanding of neurodiversity does a disservice to those with higher support needs, multiple disabilities, or intellectual disabilities. In a campaign designed to be inclusive, this exclusionary framing is itself damaging, and therefore is not something that I or many other neurodivergent people and thinkers share with Singer.[7]

The use of labels that speak in this way, in terms of levels of functioning, still persists today, but many people, both inside and outside the autistic community, reject it, and I would like to explain why.[8] To begin with, much of this usage is connected to the idea of a standardised intelligence – something that is being constantly debated because of the tendency for intelligence to be both historically and culturally determined. For the same reason that the education system cannot always be relied on for an accurate picture of a child's learning, it is very difficult to construct a clearly defined notion of intelligence.

Even if it were possible to paint a clear picture of a person's intelligence, that does not always characterise the person's ability to learn and practise the daily living skills that shape our everyday life. It also works on the assumption that each person's abilities remain in a constant state throughout their lifetime. This does not take into account the perpetual shifts we all go through, or the impact of outside factors; and it makes no allowance for people's fluctuating support needs, generating an unrealistic picture that can block access to services.

As someone who is considered 'high-functioning', many of these expectations have echoed through the responses I have received after sharing my diagnosis over the years. I have often been told that my autism 'must be really mild'. I do not object to these assumptions; as a speaking autistic white woman who is able to work, it is undeniable that I hold a huge amount of privilege. It is often easy for my autism to go undetected, and I am therefore able to avoid some of the more potent forms of ableism. Beyond medical settings, any decision to disclose my diagnosis is a matter of choice on my part – an enormous privilege that is not afforded to all.

I have not always been considered a 'productive' member of society. There were a few years when I rarely left my house or got out of bed, let alone held down a job. I have been in and out of therapy for a decade. And I have experienced episodes of autistic burnout from trying my hardest to hide my autistic traits and fit in among my neurotypical peers. For these reasons, I can understand why those labelled 'high-functioning' might find the term suffocating, and feel ashamed when they go through periods when their support needs increase.

While the term 'high-functioning' can put autistic people under a lot of pressure never to be in need of help, 'low-functioning' can also be hurtful, or an easy way to dismiss what kind of life a person can have – and, more importantly, how much joy they can fill it with.[9] Deciding that someone is 'low-functioning' may amount to deciding that there is no possible way that they can learn new skills or find new interests, shutting them into a box that will inevitably shape the course of their life. It also reveals biases around dominant forms of communication. Parents of non-speaking autistic people report that there is very little support offered for augmentative and alternative communication.[10]

In many instances, autistic people who are categorised as 'low-functioning' receive the harshest forms of mistreatment and ableism. Many report experiences of being treated as less than human, or that their inability to work means that they have been branded as a 'burden' on society.

In response to these concerns, it has become more accepted to describe an autistic person's experiences in terms of their support needs, which limits the judgements attached to a person's needs, and also allows for the natural fluctuations that shape a person's life.[11] But it is important to note that not everyone likes the phrase 'support needs', and there is always room to seek more fitting language.

This is, of course, a deeply nuanced conversation that is likely to continue for some time. Labels that explore the various experiences of autistic people are always at risk of being weaponised. If those using these terms attach value judgements to them, then we will always run the risk of pitting one group against another — especially if those value judgements are held up against capitalist ideas of what makes a 'good' human life. Discussions around labels invoking levels of functioning already constitute the cause of many rifts in the autistic community, as the struggle continues to find language that feels less dehumanising.

Many autistic advocates do not believe in the use of sublabels such as 'profound autism', and researchers have already explained the dangers behind these terms.[12] There have also been assurances given that anti-ableist language is 'fully compatible with high-quality autism research'.[13]

I do believe in ensuring that the work we do around autism does not privilege certain voices over others. But I also believe we can achieve this without falling prey to language that may be co-opted by those with ableist intentions. We should find ways to communicate all types of experiences and presentations without using one against the other, as it will help ensure that research and support is constructed in the service of *all* autistic people.

As many states fail to offer adequate help for any of the challenges faced by autistic people, highlighting our differences becomes an easy scapegoat for it to fall back on. By driving us further apart and participating in what Mary Doherty calls 'weaponized heterogeneity', we risk harming the most vulnerable among us.[14] Doherty explains how our segregation causes us to lose access to the insights gained about the experiences we share as a group. By attempting to sort us into subgroups, she writes, those with higher support needs risk losing access to the benefits of research led by autistic people specifically – research that is likely to be less dehumanising, more collaborative, and more understanding of the challenges faced.

Language can have violent consequences, and this is the place from which the issues behind functioning labels arise. Maybe we have yet to develop the language that accurately captures the breadth of support needs while also not putting anyone at risk of mistreatment. By shifting shared narratives about autistic people to those centred around care and acceptance rather than pathologisation and segregation, we will perhaps find language that fits.

Whatever happens, we should act in such a way as to support what Doherty calls the 'shared goal of improved outcomes for all autistic people'.[15]

The myriad of experiences common to neurodivergent people is one of the largest points of contention for the neurodiversity campaign. In order to understand the framework I use for my arguments, it is important that I address this here. I understand that, because of the breadth of support needs present among autistic people specifically and neurodivergent people more widely, there is a concern that the neurodiversity campaign leaves those with higher support needs or learning disabilities behind. There is a worry that the campaign can only represent those deemed 'high-functioning', like myself.

I want to emphasise that, firstly, I do not and cannot speak for all neurodivergent people. Secondly, the neurodiversity campaign that I believe in and use to inform this book does not, and should not, leave anyone behind. It should not seek to erase anyone's struggles or ignore the fact that life as a neurodivergent person is not always easy. Just because I believe every child born is deserving of love, care and safety, and that no one deserves to be subject to eugenics, that does not mean I believe in ignoring disability, or that I am ignorant of how difficult it must be to care for someone who is not valued by the world around them. I hope that the arguments I share convey that I believe higher support needs do not exclude anyone from the right to exist free from discrimination and violence, or the right to have the world around them rebuilt to accommodate and support them and their families.

Once the rise of internet chat rooms connected autistic people to one another, Singer was able to follow the development of their budding identity and the similarities between their shared experiences, and to issue a call for a campaign that supported their shared desires for acceptance and support.

She writes in her thesis that her work aligns with the aims of emancipatory research, locating it once again in a political sphere. She enumerates the following characteristics from Colin Barnes and Geoff Mercer's introduction to *Doing Disability Research*:

- Open partnership on the side of the oppressed, and political commitment to their causes.
- Rejection of claims to objectivity and neutrality on the grounds that all knowledge is socially constructed and culturally relative.
- Motivated by the need to change the world, not simply describe it – not only the social and material conditions of disabled people, but also the relations of research production.
- Reflexive recognition of the power difference that exists between researchers and researched in order to ensure that the outcome is enabling and not disabling.[16]

Like any political movement, the neurodiversity campaign has grown substantially, with its core emancipatory aims expanding way beyond Singer's original aims and now seeking to confront the social oppression of those whose existence is at odds with neuroconformity.

By opening up the neurodiversity campaign to a wider range of diagnoses and experiences, we can broaden the question of the ways in which the world is not set up to cope with variations in cognition, and what can be done about it.

Each individual diagnosis will bring its own specific challenges, of course – but there are also many overlaps in the positive changes that can be made. Acceptance, understanding and destigmatisation stand out as the most important. Opposing the medical pathologisation of individuals with these diagnoses means imagining a world that is so accessible, where so much support is provided upon request, that eventually these diagnoses themselves become defunct, because the question is no longer, 'What is it about you that is supposedly at odds with our world?', but instead, 'What support do you need today to live your life?'

Singer's original vision for neurodiversity has, appropriately, changed with the growing needs of people around the world. An emerging vision for neurodiversity rejects the alienation and ostracisation that so many neurodivergent and disabled people have faced in the past, instead considering how we might build a world for every type of life.

Different Approaches Are No Bad Thing

In an emerging movement, it is no secret that there is an abundance of conflicting ideas within discussions of neurodiversity, and that this may have contributed to the co-opting and watering down of the term itself. As Ari Ne'eman and Elizabeth Pellicano note, this even affects the use of the word 'neurodiversity' itself. Some believe that the term registers a strict biological fact – that neurodiversity exists within the human population and must be accepted – while others believe it to be purely ideological and related only to a political position.

Having multiple 'neurodiversity approaches', in Patrick Dwyer's terms, is not necessarily a bad thing. It promotes debate within communities and allows for the discussion of a multitude of ideas and action points. It does, however, make a narrowing of focus more difficult.

A large part of these discussions revolve around what may be considered the core tenet of neurodiversity: the rejection of any proposed 'cure'. At the heart of neurodiversity is the belief that neurodivergent people do not deserve to be eradicated or 'cured' of their 'afflictions'.

This preference for understanding neurodivergence through a social model of disability does not mean that the model itself is perfect, as many have pointed out. Some have suggested that it can lead to the dismissal of hardships that are less related to environmental factors.

As Dwyer notes, there is still the possibility that, even with all societal barriers removed, disabled people would still face particular struggles. He provides the example that 'someone who struggles with executive function might still encounter time management challenges even if they have access to scheduling apps and accommodations'.[17] He also suggests that the social model's focus on environmental changes may lead to the rejection of things like the teaching of new skills to disabled people who want to learn them, which may in turn prevent disabled people from fulfilling their aspirations. Dwyer suggests that, because of the nuance involved here, a neurodiversity approach that occupies a middle ground is perhaps a good alternative.

This kind of approach assumes that the state of being disabled arises from a dynamic interplay between the individual characteristics of a disabled person and the surrounding context in which they live. The objective should never be to cure or 'normalise' the disabled person.[18] Disability can be addressed either by modifying societal and environmental factors (such as reducing discriminatory attitudes) or by enhancing an individual's capabilities (such as teaching them new skills). The variety of brains and minds that exist should be valued, and those with cognitive disabilities embraced and respected as they are.

This approach may allow for individuals to seek support for coping with certain traits related to their diagnosis without putting an onus on the individual to eradicate their neurodivergence, and without reducing the demand on the wider society to make accommodations.

An example of this can be seen in my own experience with self-harm. Autistic people are thought to experience a substantially increased risk of self-harm in comparison to non-autistic people, studies suggesting that their likelihood of self-harming is three times higher.[19] I self-harmed for six years, and I believe this was related to the mental health difficulties I experienced as an undiagnosed autistic person. I have never felt any desire to 'cure' my autism, but I did ask for help to stop self-harming. I was given access to skills to help me cope with this need, as well as support to understand where the desire to hurt myself was coming from. This is not something that everyone is able to access; I was lucky to have received this help, and for it to have been successful. There is, however, the question of whether I would ever have started self-harming at all, or had the mental health crises I did, if there had been a better societal understanding of autism, and I had had access to support earlier on.

This nuanced approach may provide neurodivergent individuals with the autonomy to decide what they want their life to look like without the constant emergence of societal barriers. It does not disavow the idea that society causes the majority of issues for disabled individuals, but it may also provide a helpful alternative for those who feel their disability extends beyond any accommodations that might be made. It might shift the focus onto encouraging support, so long as the people involved do not experience it as an attempt to cure something that is at the core of their being.

The final model I want to summarise here is one advanced by Robert Chapman. He suggests that in the context of neurodiversity it may be helpful to refer to Elizabeth Barnes's value-neutral model. Though it was originally proposed for physical disabilities, Chapman suggests that this model may allow for those with cognitive disabilities to be honest about the good, bad and neutral dimensions of their disability – and that the disabilities themselves are not inherently good or bad, but rather made one or the other by extraneous factors.

Chapman proposes that the application of this model might be best understood through the example of autism. Studies have long suggested that autistic people are likely to experience a lower quality of life than the non-autistic population – low levels of 'well-being', in terms of Barnes's model. This has led to the assumption that autism itself is the culprit – hence the desire to eradicate it. But Chapman counters this with a 2006 study that found that, rather than being a function of how 'severe' their autism was, an autistic person's well-being was directly linked to 'whether they felt supported (in other words, it was determined by the external context, not where on the spectrum any individual was)'.[20]

Chapman also suggests that, rather than painting a cognitive disability as wholly good or wholly bad, we can consider whether the experience of these disabilities is affected by a person's other cognitive traits. Chapman highlights the example of Down syndrome, citing a 2011 well-being study that suggested that people in this group were likely to experience 'strikingly high' levels of happiness. This led Chapman to suggest that their well-being might also be conditioned by their cognitive profile – and in this case it was the cognitive disability itself that was positively contributing to well-being.

This leaves room for some nuance. The demonisation of forms of neurodivergence, and widespread assumptions about the value of a life with certain diagnoses, contributes to discrimination, stigma and, as Chapman proves, group well-being. One can therefore argue that the quality of life of a neurodivergent individual is largely determined by other factors than the diagnosis itself. We have in our power the possibility of controlling and improving these factors.

Note that Chapman does not attempt to avoid the fact that there are likely to be cases in which a number of traits do push an individual towards lower levels of well-being, but asserts that Barnes's model predicts these examples. The propensity for certain individuals to experience low levels of well-being is, according to Chapman, no more frequent in those with cognitive disabilities than those without. There are, after all, many people in the world who are unhappy and are neither neurodivergent nor disabled.

The benefit of the value-neutral model is that it allows neurodivergent people to give realistic accounts of their experiences without deeming them automatically responsible because they were born one way rather than another. It does not write off people whose lives look one way rather than another. It takes into account the importance of external treatment but does not ignore the breadth of internal experiences.

As Chapman suggests, using this model 'may help provide a more direct challenge to the depiction of cognitive disability as tragic and at odds with the good human life'.[21] Perhaps this itself gets to the heart of the neurodiversity campaign, by engaging the argument that we have no right to diminish certain lives and declare them worthless. By expanding our understanding of a 'good' life, we may challenge the oppressive norms that have led until now to the dismissal and mistreatment of neurodivergent people.

Now, More than Ever

Today, the number of individuals receiving neurodivergent diagnoses is steadily increasing. As a greater number of people begin to understand themselves through this framework, many are receiving diagnoses but then being left with none of the support or resources they need.

While conversations around neurodiversity are proliferating, they seem to have little impact on the deep-rooted ideas that shape these diagnoses. As we have seen, it has been historically common to treat neurodivergent people as a group who should be separated from the rest of society and subjected to attempts to 'fix' them.

The most recent studies on trauma and neurodivergence suggest that people with 'high autistic traits' have a 30 per cent chance of having endured severe trauma throughout their life that leads to PTSD symptoms: this is more than three times the percentage for those without any such traits (8 per cent).[22] This study, like so many before it, clearly demonstrates that being neurodivergent puts you at risk of mistreatment and much more. But it is crucial to point out here that this trauma comes at the hands of others – others who often do not respect neurodivergent people or believe them worthy of care.

While many may assume that this mistreatment will be at the hands of those who simply do not understand neurodivergence, and therefore do not know any better, studies of the treatment of autistic people in scholarly research proves otherwise. Working as an autistic academic and community psychologist, Monique Botha explores the construction of autistic people in autism research. Declaring that 'autism research is in crisis', Botha reports on the prevalence of dehumanising descriptions and objectifying treatment of autistic people by autism researchers.[23] Botha's research highlights a distinct attempt at 'othering' autistic people, not unlike the construction of 'otherness' used to dominate other marginalised groups throughout history. Botha states that 'autistic people have been compared to non-human animals and described as less domesticated than non-autistic people, described as lacking in agency, rationality, epistemic authority, the ability to form community or share culture.'[24]

Given how much academic research informs public policy, and that academic 'experts' are relied upon to share their opinions with the general public, it is fair to suggest that the values present in research – and the language that shapes them – make themselves felt beyond the academy. Often turned to as a site for producing shared knowledge, academic research is seen as trustworthy and used to justify actions that affect all of us. If the attitudes Botha highlights dominate the discussions around autism, then their impact is potentially devastating.

One of the central aims of the neurodiversity campaign is to tackle the way in which neurodivergence is understood. We can improve the lives of neurodivergent people by reducing stigma, increasing respect, and changing the view that we are always in some way deficient. The potential benefits of such changes will be greatly enhanced when they are deployed to affect material differences and structural changes, as well as cultural ones.

The Covid-19 pandemic provides a striking example of the need for progress within the neurodiversity campaign. The pandemic and its subsequent impact upon communities around the world shone a dismal light on the inequalities that plague our societies. Cracks that already existed widened under the weight of such devastation.

In the largest mass-disabling event in decades, the United States alone reported an estimated 1.2 million more people registering as disabled in the space of just a year as a result of the virus.[25] A sudden surge in the need for disability support demonstrated just how poorly so many of the systems across the world were set up to aid disabled people, as well as exposing the flimsy basis of able-bodied supremacy. This was a reminder that able-bodiedness is not a secure, fixed state; nor is it guaranteed, given that most people will at some point in their life face an experience of disability, whether temporary or permanent.[26]

Data suggests that the majority of those who lost their lives to Covid-19 were disabled, and that, though disabled people were disproportionately affected by the pandemic, they were often forgotten about in policy plans. In England, reports showed that six out of ten deaths were disabled people.[27] This pattern was reflected in many countries, such as the US and China, who completed extensive enquiries into the handling of the pandemic and its effect on the lives of disabled people.[28] This highlights the poor treatment disabled people frequently receive, and the ways in which they are often treated as disposable.

The treatment of autistic people and other neurodivergent people, in particular, was brought under scrutiny when reports were published that claimed many autistic people and people with learning disabilities in the UK were being automatically labelled with blanket Do Not Resuscitate orders (DNRs), without any consultation with the individual or their family.[29]

Those with learning disabilities were found to experience a death rate 4.1 times higher than that of the rest of the population.[30] The UK social care sector was reportedly left to fend for itself by those in charge, often being left without vital resources such as PPE. Many have reported that it became clear throughout the pandemic that autistic people and those with learning disabilities were being treated as an afterthought. The issue around blanket DNRs eventually prompted an open letter to staff in the NHS declaring that such orders were 'unacceptable'.[31] This was no doubt a PR strategy in response to the exposure of their blatant disregard for the lives of the people concerned.

It is very likely that prevalent attitudes towards neurodivergent people meant that, as soon as the crisis began, their lives held very little weight for decision-makers. Like the elderly, they were seen as an easy group to give up on – which is exactly what happened. Times of great stress offer a sobering way to determine who those in power will scramble to save. Neurodivergent people were not on that list.

At present, a diagnosis is, in most cases, the only way to access the very meagre support and resources in a person's community. But, as this discussion has shown, that does not mean that receiving an official diagnosis comes without risk. It is becoming increasingly clear that to have a diagnosis without feeling any repercussions or experiencing poor treatment as a result is in fact a privilege.

Being open about your diagnosis or having it on your medical record is more than likely to result in discrimination, particularly if you are already marginalised. In the case of autism, this discrimination is so prevalent that people like Devon Price have explained in detail why you may want to rethink seeking a diagnosis.[32]

In medical settings, neurodivergent people are often denied access to life-saving transplants on the basis of their disability. Parents have reported that doctors have told them that their children will not be put on transplant lists because they were born with Down syndrome, autism, or other cognitive disabilities.[33] The extent of this discrimination became so widespread that, in 2021, laws were passed in multiple US states to ensure that disabled people were eligible for organ transplants – laws that had been fought for by the parents of neurodivergent children whose lives were at risk.[34]

Beyond medical settings, there is also the chance that having an official diagnosis can mean you are unable to immigrate, rejected by certain governments because of the 'high cost' you may pose to the country's health system.[35] Price goes on to explain other risks, such as being forced into guardianships in which you are stripped of your autonomy, being denied access to gender-affirming care, and losing parental rights.

Much of this discrimination is systemic, present around the world, and puts autistic people at risk of abuse. It is dictated by the dangerous view of autistic people as less than human. Such discrimination is sadly far from a thing of the past.

Beyond the risks of diagnosis, it is important to recognise that, just because diagnosis is often required to access support, that does not mean that the system will work.

Diagnosis is part of what allows the medical model to thrive; it functions as the main driver behind pathologisation. The attachment of a label to a neurodivergent person may enable them to get access to a tiny amount of public resources – but they will also then be at risk of mistreatment and discrimination. The neurodiversity movement exists in opposition to this medical pathologisation and to the idea that there are 'normal' and 'non-normal' brains.

This means that one crucial goal of neurodiversity is to eliminate the need for such labels, to rid the medical model of its power. Today, the survival of many neurodivergent people is dependent upon these diagnoses – but that does not mean we should accept that as a given, or that we cannot imagine something different.

Constructing and legitimising alternatives to our current systems may seem like a terrifying or impossible prospect. There is a lot of fear attached to the thought of a sudden upheaval that changes the way our world has functioned for many years. But that does not make it a ridiculous ideal.

Consider that, through connecting the work of the neurodiversity campaign with other movements for liberation, we can create a world where, whenever necessary, anyone can gain access to the care they need. In response to this need, resources would be made automatically available to that person; and access to those resources would not be determined by wealth, age, location, gender, sexuality, race, any pre-existing access to care, or any of the other factors that currently determine people's access to adequate help. Nobody who wanted to access this care would be held back by the prospect of facing ableism, being mistreated, or experiencing discrimination.

In a world with those systems of care, would pathologisation be necessary? Can we imagine a world without these labels?

It is entirely possible that some of this language will remain in use in order to explain a person's experience of the world, to help communicate what it feels like to be in this or that body. But there is the hope that a world built in the service of liberation for all would not require us to continue giving power to systems that seek to dehumanise us, control us, and in many cases kill us. Something new can emerge.

2

NEURODIVERSITY IS
A POLITICAL ISSUE

In 2021, a study called Spectrum 10K was put on hold shortly after it had been announced. The study, led by Simon Baron-Cohen, was proposed as the largest ever UK study of autism, and was intended to collect DNA from 10,000 autistic people. It caused mass controversy in the autistic community. Many people raised their fears not only about privacy and data protection issues, but also about the possibility that the study might be used to determine an 'autism gene' that could then be detected in pregnancy, providing parents with the opportunity to abort an autistic baby.

As the number of children born with Down syndrome continues to dwindle in European countries and the United States thanks to prenatal testing, this fear is not unfounded. In 2017, Dutch newspapers came under fire when they published a letter that stated that 'the freedom to birth disabled children should be limited by the "financial burden" to society', and that because of the societal costs that arise from caring for disabled people, parents who choose not to abort disabled children should face financial consequences.[1]

While access to abortion is a fundamental right that should be afforded to every pregnant person across the globe, behind the more sinister attempts at population control stands a theory of eugenics: a set of beliefs that are by no means of contemporary origin (even Plato believed in selective mating), of which the most well-known example was pursued by Nazi Germany. Eugenics is founded on the belief that the human population can be improved by altering human gene pools to protect and nurture only those genes and people thought to be 'superior' or 'normal'. Deeply rooted in racist practices and white supremacy, these inhumane beliefs have long been thought to be a cure for society's ills, advanced by political leaders who believed eugenics to be a worthy cause. One such leader was Winston Churchill, who declared:

> The unnatural and increasingly rapid growth of the feeble-minded and insane classes, coupled as it is with steady restriction among all the thrifty, energetic and superior stocks constitutes a national and race danger which it is impossible to exaggerate. I feel that the source from which the stream of madness is fed should be cut off and sealed off before another year has passed.[2]

As well as being used to further racist aims, eugenics has often been applied to disabled people and those with mental illnesses, who have historically been deemed 'unfit' citizens, and many of them were sterilised without their knowledge. During the twentieth century this led to the forced sterilisation of as many as 70,000 Americans, many of whom were people of colour, and the victims included those who 'had been labelled "mentally deficient," as well as those who were deaf, blind, and diseased'.[3]

These sterilisations were sanctioned by law after the Supreme Court passed *Buck v. Bell* in 1927. In his comment on the law, Justice Holmes claimed that the 'feebleminded' in question 'sap the strength of the state' and were therefore worthy sacrifices. Despite almost a century having passed, this language is all but identical to the arguments we see today that suggest disabled people are a 'burden' because of their needs.

This highlights the resilience of the prejudice against disabled people. Justice Holmes's message continues, 'It is better for the world if, instead of waiting to execute degenerate offspring for crime or to let them starve for their imbecility, society can prevent those who are manifestly unfit from continuing their kind.'[4]

A key moment in the history of systemic ableism, *Buck v. Bell* contributed to a form of discrimination that continues to strip disabled people of their agency and devalue their lives today. As I write, in 2023, the statute has yet to be overturned.[5]

Unfortunately, in countries such as Australia, the non-consensual sterilisation of disabled women and girls remains a legal practice.[6] Moreover, as I will show, conception is not the only instance in which disabled people's lives remain at risk from those who believe eugenics to be a worthwhile objective.

While some may say that eugenics is a thing of the past, and that studies such as Spectrum 10K do not pose a threat to disabled people, it is clear that the opposite is true – especially given that the leader of the study, Simon Baron-Cohen, has said previously that, when conducting DNA studies on autism, 'there's no way that we can ever say that a future political leader or a scientist won't use the research for eugenics'.[7]

However, while the potential for dangerous attitudes towards neurodivergent people remains high, the reaction to the study provides a glimpse of hope for the growing rejection of these attitudes. The study garnered much public attention, as many believed it to be an infringement of various human rights – the rights to life, to privacy and to freedom from discrimination being most at risk. Organising together as a community, people held protests in front of centres that were scheduled to take part in the study, and organised a campaign, Boycott Spectrum 10K, which gained the support of thousands of people, and held panels to discuss the issues with the study as a community.

The successful halting of the study, prompting an investigation from an ethics agency (which sadly gave the study a green light to continue), demonstrates that the neurodiversity campaign does have an effective politic dimension, and that its aims are rooted in rejecting the dehumanisation of neurodivergent people.

Neurodiversity rejects the alienation and ostracisation of anyone who is deemed to exist outside the scope of medical 'norms', refusing the coercion of any individual towards those norms. Jesse Meadows, writer and host of the *Disorderland* podcast, explains that we must not ignore neurodiversity's opposition to binaries: '[Neurodiversity] is not a nice euphemism for autism, and it's about far more than just fighting negative connotations. Neurodiversity is a paradigm, a lens through which we look at human neurology, and it stands in opposition to the pathology paradigm.'[8]

This paradigm opposes every medical quest for a 'cure', asking us to think about what it means to decide that ridding the world of a minority group is a positive or worthwhile goal. As Nick Chown explains, 'No valid case has yet been made that the health of the social body requires the amputation of the autistic parts of the body.'[9] What do people hope to gain through the eradication of autism or neurodivergence? What will the world lose if that aim is ever achieved? Who has the authority to decide which lives deserve to be lived?

Understanding autism and neurodiversity as deficits reinforces what is considered 'normal' in society – a concept that has defined our social lives for as long as humans have existed. It is the socially constructed hierarchy of human existence that creates the imbalances of power that so many people are affected by today. Rich vs poor, man vs woman vs nonbinary person, heterosexual vs homosexual, neurotypical vs neuroatypical – these are all categories that are awarded cultural value and used to justify (or ignore) oppressive treatment. Neurodiversity offers us the opportunity to subvert these norms – specifically, to subvert neuronormativity. It allows us to question and destabilise the fantasy that there are 'normal' and 'abnormal' ways of thinking and being.

☙

By looking to the past we can see how much of this pathologisation has come into play in the service of capitalism. Exploring the politics of mental health and the creation of asylums, Micha Frazer-Carroll explains that the Industrial Revolution forced many 'Mad/Mentally Ill' and disabled people (and therefore also neurodivergent people) out of the house and into asylums.[10] Unable to meet the demands of the factory and unable to be cared for by family members who could no longer work from the home, these groups of people were used to fill the publicly funded mental asylums that, in the UK, were mandated by the passing of two Asylum Acts.

This, as Frazer-Carroll writes, became 'a way of managing poor, disabled, and unruly bodyminds that could not be easily exploited for profit'.[11] As the state began to facilitate the 'care' of these people, it needed a categorisation that could determine who should be locked away and who should not, who could be sent to work and who could not. This forced binary meant, as Frazer-Carroll states, that 'the line between Madness and sanity became dependent on the capitalist mode of production and managed by the state'.[12] This regulation of the population paved the way for a medical-industrial complex that serves to position neurodivergence as a deviance from the norm, as well as continuing to categorise the population based on their ability to perform labour.

Non-conformity in the context of the social order reveals the non-conformist as a problem to be dealt with. Despite the mass closure of asylums and psychiatric hospitals across the United States and the UK during the end of the twentieth century, mad, disabled, and neurodivergent people continue to be locked up and kept away, albeit by different means.

Neurodiversity and Abolition

In the UK, reports suggest that half of all those entering prisons are neurodivergent.[13] Despite the fact that research has dispelled myths such as autistic people being more likely to commit crimes, we come into contact with the criminal justice system at disproportionate rates.[14] The nature of these interactions is most concerning, with a huge number resulting in violence and fatality in both the UK and the United States.

In 2016, an analysis of the deaths of those killed by law enforcement in the United States suggested that up to half of the people who lost their lives had a cognitive disability.[15] To be a person of colour or otherwise marginalised significantly exacerbates this risk, as the example of Elijah McClain demonstrates. An autistic man who was walking home from the corner shop, he died at the hands of officers who claimed he 'matched the description' of someone who had been reported for strange behaviour. Restrained and injected with ketamine, Elijah died as a result of excessive force from officers who refused to listen to his pleas that he had done nothing wrong.[16]

The UK fares little better. With autistic people reportedly facing high levels of police discrimination,[17] the Metropolitan Police came under fire in the early 2000s for a situation in which a non-speaking, autistic sixteen-year-old boy with epilepsy had been brutally restrained and handcuffed by seven officers while at a swimming pool.[18] Terrified by being forced face down onto the ground and forcibly restrained against his will, the teenager was later diagnosed with post-traumatic stress disorder, and it was found that his epilepsy had worsened.

As the research conducted has yet to find any justifiable reason why neurodivergent people are disproportionately represented in the criminal justice system, writers like Robert Chapman suggest we can only assume that it is the result of structural failings in an ableist society, which create a systemic problem that is compounded by other forms of marginalisation.[19]

The gravity of these systemic failings is what brings us to a line of political thinking that can be found within many conversations about neurodiversity: abolition. So much of what neurodiversity demands of us is the dismantling, rethinking and reimagining of systems, norms and processes that have long dominated our world. For this reason, the politics of abolition can work in tandem with the ideas behind neurodiversity.

In the context of policing and the criminal justice system, it is clear that these institutions are failing neurodivergent people and putting lives at risk in the process. Given that neurodivergent people are dehumanised, abused and incarcerated at staggering rates, the abolition of these systems seems crucial for their liberation.

But moving beyond the realm of the policing and incarceration systems, these politics give us the opportunity to think also of abolishing capitalism, racism, imperialism, the patriarchy, and every other system that works against a future in which we are *all* liberated.

Entering mainstream discourse in 2020, calls to abolish the police arose in tandem with the Black Lives Matter movement and its organisation of uprisings during that year. Perhaps best known for this work is Angela Davis, who has written about her radical visions for the future and the politics of abolition feminism. Abolition feminism can be described as working to develop strategies that free us from both structural and interpersonal violence and confront all forms of oppression and their intersecting natures. Following the collective work of two organisations – INCITE! Women of Color Against Violence and Critical Resistance – a joint statement written in 2001 contained the following:

> We seek to build movements that not only end violence, but that create a society based on radical freedom, mutual accountability, and passionate reciprocity. In this society, safety and security will not be premised on violence or the threat of violence; it will be based on a collective commitment to guaranteeing the survival and care of all peoples.[20]

The continuing incarceration of neurodivergent people demonstrates how systemically neurological non-conformity is viewed as a type of criminality that should be controlled and kept hidden away. By merging the politics behind both neurodiversity and abolition, we can resist this tendency.

Carceral systems, the police and the law in their current manifestations fail marginalised groups, unfairly targeting them and exposing them to unending violence. Neurodivergent people are undoubtedly victims of this state of affairs. By demanding that society deal with the ways current systems are failing, abolition can help us to consider what are the most pressing needs of neurodivergent people.

Two examples are experiences of sexual violence and the risk of psychiatric detention. A terrifying statistic brought to light in discussing abolition and neurodiversity comes from the United States, where those with intellectual disabilities are *seven* times more likely to be sexually assaulted than those without.[21] Often occurring in institutions and group homes by people the victims have been taught to trust, the majority of these assaults go unprosecuted and unaddressed, leading to repeat offences.

What does it say about the efficacy of our current systems that this group of people are exploited and abused by those who claim to care for them, before being forced to forgo any meaningful justice because of their continued marginalisation? What would a specialised service built in aid of survivors look like? What would it require to build support systems that keep neurodivergent people out of institutions and away from those who dehumanise and abuse the people they are charged to protect?

To consider the impact of psychiatric detention, we can look back to Frazer-Carroll's work. Discussing this other form of institutionalisation, she highlights the number of autistic people and people with learning disabilities who are detained in hospitals under the Mental Health Act, explaining that, for this group, the average length of a hospital stay is 5.4 years, while more than half are detained for more than 2 years.[22] In 2021, the BBC reported that, in England, 100 people with learning disabilities and autism had been held in institutions for at least 20 years.[23]

While psychiatric detention and hospital stays in assessment and treatment units are currently looked upon as forms of support for those who need them, those who have been held under the Mental Health Act (1983) or admitted because of their complex needs report experiencing hostile treatment that is not unlike that of a prison environment. Heavy restraint practices, restrictions on moving around the hospital, and degrading treatment from those tasked with the care of patients are among the horrors that often await those who find themselves admitted. The mother of an autistic man who was 'fed through a hatch' and denied physical contact in a hospital in Cheshire even considered legal action because of the poor quality of life that was being provided for her son. 'People wouldn't treat an animal as badly,' she said.[24]

Unfortunately, scandals of this kind are not uncommon. In fact, every few years it seems that a report on the harrowing conditions at a UK care home or mental health facility are revealed. In the 1980s a documentary, *Silent Minority*, was released; it looked at the lives of those in two hospitals, in Reading and Surrey.[25] Some years later, the Winterbourne View scandal saw six staff members at a care home jailed for their abuse of disabled patients.[26] And in 2021 the level of care in a Kent home for those with learning disabilities and autism became so poor that families were given just ten hours' notice before it was shut down completely – a move that the family of one resident called 'inhumane'.[27]

The expansive nature of abolition politics encourages us not only to find ways to reorganise our society to ensure the horrifying details of cases like this become a thing of the past, but also to question what this continued incarceration of neurodivergent people means for how we view those who 'dissent' in society. Why does existing in a way that diverges from the norm render you at risk of imprisonment and violence? Why do we seek to lock people away when they do not meet our standards of neuroconformity? What resources should we focus on building to keep people with their loved ones, and how do we reject these various forms of segregation? How can we ensure that neurodivergent people are not stripped of their autonomy?

Politicising our understanding of neurodiversity requires us to confront the ways in which our institutions, workplaces, homes, schools, universities and more all create social demands that must be complied with if we are to avoid outing ourselves as 'dysfunctional' and being deemed worthy of locking away.

Neurodiversity can successfully align with abolition through its direct rejection of our society's tendency to view certain lives as disposable. Ruth Wilson Gilmore, a prominent thinker and worker in abolitionist spaces, believes that freedom is a physical, tangible place. For her, this means 'we combine resources, ingenuity, and commitment to produce the conditions in which

life is precious for all'.[28] For me, this should be a guiding prin-
ciple for neurodiversity and the ways in which it can liberate us.

Rejecting Commodification

The politics of neurodiversity demand that we locate it beyond
the realm of the personal, and this requires an exploration
of how ableism operates in the broader contexts of racism,
capitalism, prisons, and so on. Such an exploration requires us
to question the authority of medical systems that have sought
to lock up, punish, and kill neurodivergent people, and why
these medical systems are still seen as essential in validating
our own experience of the world through diagnosis.

If we are to maintain the political dimension of neurodiversity, as was intended by those who first articulated the idea, then
there is reason to resist the commodification of these experiences that has become increasingly prominent: the creation of
products promising, in one way or another, to optimise your
experience – programmes that will turn your ADHD into a
'superpower' or suggest that you can be a girl-boss autistic
CEO if you follow 'these five tips'.

An unsurprising phenomenon given capitalism's ability to
commodify anything and everything, this kind of neurodiversity presents each experience as completely individualised
and disconnected from a wider community, as well as failing
to question the structural issues that people face on a day-to-
day level.

One threat that arises here comes from the amplification

of the most 'sellable' parts of neurodivergence. Those who are considered most marketable are those who are most often amplified, resulting in a surge of neurodivergent representation that is white, middle-class, English-speaking, and considered non-threatening and palatable by much of the wider population. The elevation of this narrow section of neurodivergent people means that an additional expectation is placed upon neurodivergent people to behave this way. When they fail to do so – as doing so is, of course, impossible – this creates a risk of further marginalisation. 'I support neurodivergent people but not neurodivergent people who behave in a way that I deem unpalatable' means that any chance at liberation becomes fragmented, derailed once again by discrimination.

By allowing our vision of neurodiversity to be infiltrated by the insidious nature of capitalism, we risk losing sight of the aim to liberate *all* neurodivergent people. This form of neurodiversity can and will abandon people. Those neurodivergent people who cannot be exploited under capitalism because of their inability to work will be at risk of being forgotten, their neurodivergence unable to be harnessed for profit.

I have no qualms about the use of self-empowerment practices for a population of people who are so frequently demonised and alienated, but I do think that failing to demand more from our understanding of neurodiversity brings a halt to what we can achieve. By refusing the hyperindividualism that already plagues so much of the Western world, we can turn instead towards more liberatory practices.

Instead of hiring an ADHD coach who teaches you to be

maximally productive at work, consider whether the way we currently work is in fact detrimental to us as social beings. Why have we normalised tying how much we work to the kind of life we 'deserve'? Instead of creating pseudoscientific tips for forcing nonspeaking people into communicating verbally, consider why we have decided to prioritise one form of communication over every other. Why are we not doing more to develop and provide (for free!) alternative forms of communication that work for those who need them.

Neurodiversity can be liberating in its refusal to simply accept things as they are, and its push to question the way our world currently functions. By individualising our experiences of neurodivergence, we might overlook this, and as a result neglect the consequences of phenomena that control our experiences as a whole, such as the impact of ableism.

Ableism (which I will return to in Chapter 3) can contribute to phenomena such as Damian Milton's 'double empathy problem'.[29] A seminal work in autistic advocacy circles, Milton's essay deals with autistic people's supposed 'deficiency' in social communication. He observes that, while autistic people are presumed to lack 'theory of mind', and are therefore seen as unable to imagine the thoughts and feelings of others or predict their behaviour, non-autistic people fail to make much effort towards understanding autistic ways of thinking and being.

This makes the problem of empathy and understanding one that functions both ways, and not something that stems simply from autistic people's 'deficient' cognition. More recent research suggests that autistic peer-to-peer information transfer is highly effective, but that neurotypical peers are less willing to interact with autistic people due to negative judgements they make about them.[30] It is in such breakdowns in communication that we can begin to question the impact of ableism.

Among such misunderstandings and struggles in communication, how many are caused by a lack of interest in understanding how somebody different to you understands the world? And how much of that attitude is fuelled by an ableist perception of autistic people being deficient in some way, and therefore not worth the trouble of empathy? Preconceived judgements and stigma towards autistic people restrict societal attempts to interact with and include them, so that autistic people find themselves socially marginalised.

Understanding these situations through the lens of pathology suggests that autistic people should be taught that their most natural or innate form of communication is faulty, and that it is their responsibility to learn how to change their behaviour to fit in. Under the neurodiversity paradigm, we might ask: Why have we created a hierarchy that normalises some social interaction and communication styles and alienates others? Who is served by the dominant or 'normal' form, and who is left behind?

If we retain only this commodified form of neurodiversity we risk losing the chance to consider the ways in which being neurodivergent can interact with one's other identities and life experiences. It might keep us from performing what critical race theorist Mari Matsuda called 'ask[ing] the other question'. In 1991, Matsuda wrote:

> When I see something that looks racist, I ask, 'Where is the patriarchy in this?' When I see something that looks sexist, I ask, 'Where is the heterosexism in this?' When I see something that looks homophobic, I ask, 'Where are the class interests in this?' Working in coalition forces us to look for both the obvious and the nonobvious forms of domination, and, as we have done this, we have come to see that no form of subordination ever stands alone.[31]

In the context of neurodiversity, working with intersectional politics like these ensures that the emergence of the movement can move in tandem with constantly shifting political needs. Instead of becoming diluted by its sudden rise in popularity neurodiversity must instead remain ever-evolving.

One article that might be considered to 'ask the other question' is by Licia Carlson, who used feminist concepts to analyse the history of cognitive disability in the United States throughout the nineteenth and twentieth centuries.[32] While the arguments she advanced may be outdated, they can be brought into a more contemporary setting to understand how marginalised groups have always experienced neurodivergence in various ways.

She begins by noting the ways in which the treatment and

classification of women with cognitive disabilities was markedly different than that of men, explaining that popular gender stereotypes of the time influenced how institutions defined and dealt with these women. During this period, a general fear prevailed that these women would bear illegitimate children, and therefore needed their sexual expression controlled – something that aligned with the forced sterilisations mentioned earlier in this chapter.

While the issue of reproduction seems less of a preoccupation today, we can nevertheless see how existing as anything other than a cisgender man may continue to directly impact your experience of neurodivergence. Some have attributed this to the fact that early studies into autism involved a majority of male participants, while others suspect it relates to the societal expectations that are culturally attached to different genders, and a few believe it is a function of the prominence of highly contested hypotheses such as Simon Baron-Cohen's 'extreme male brain theory'.

Whatever the case, we can see that having a marginalised identity may still lead to one's neurodivergence being overlooked or met with misconceptions. A recent estimate for the Australian population suggested that 80 per cent of girls remained undiagnosed at the age of eighteen, which matches my own experience.[33] However, Devon Price has illustrated that it is unlikely these discrepancies are related solely to gender, and should instead be understood as affecting anyone who is socially marginalised. This explains why research shows that access to timely diagnosis is also affected by race.[34] This means that many autistic people of colour are less likely to receive suitable post-diagnosis support, or that their parents may not be provided with prompt access to necessary resources.

Carlson explores the various ways in which cognitive disabilities have always had a complicated relationship to motherhood.

In the context of autism, this is vividly illustrated by the popularity of Leo Kanner's (now abandoned) term 'refrigerator mothers' from the 1940s. It described a process in which a mother was so cold and uncaring towards her child that they developed autism as a result.

While the fear of disabled women producing illegitimate children, or of women producing disability through their own 'failed' motherhood, was a cause for concern at the time, that does not mean that institutions did not also exploit women for their assumed caretaking abilities.

Carlson explains that, from the very beginning, institutions that housed disabled people relied upon women's labour, to the extent that female patients were tasked with caring for other patients. It is unsurprising that this vision of women as exploitable caretakers persisted even when the women themselves had been kept away from society for being 'defective'. As Carlson explains, 'Though in need of segregation and protection by virtue of her deficient intellect and moral faculty, the "feebleminded" woman's caregiving nature remained intact.'[35]

By viewing this history from a feminist perspective, we can see the way in which women with cognitive disabilities were not only subject to oppressive stereotypes regarding their character, but also excluded from society in institutions. They were exploited in order to provide a form of labour for which they were deemed suitable under the watchful eyes of those who ran the institutions. As Carlson writes, 'Her labor served the needs of the very structure that limited her freedom.'[36]

The past continues to be reflected in our present. We must ensure that we do not continue to marginalise neurodivergent people on the basis of their gender. This may involve combating underdiagnosis, ensuring better post-diagnosis support, extending research into neurodivergent experiences of gender, or indeed working to protect and provide gender-affirmative care.

3

NEURODIVERSITY AND DISABILITY JUSTICE

In 2021 a US court decided to allow electric shock devices to be used in a school for disabled children and adults, many of whom are autistic or have intellectual disabilities.[1] It was argued that this might successfully modify behaviour such as self-harm. In contrast, those who sought to ban the devices described their use as 'torture' and argued that the use of the shocks is often excessive and carries the risk of causing lasting damage. The FDA reported that there was 'weak' evidence that the treatment was effective, but the court chose to overturn the ban anyway, possibly influenced by the quarter-million dollars spent on lobbying by the school during the past decade. Many of those who took to Twitter to condemn the ruling with the hashtag #StopTheShocks compared this treatment of autistic people to the use of shock collars on dogs and cattle prods on livestock, reminding us that autistic people are considered by some to be less than human.

Electric shock treatment for autistic children has been conducted for some time, and it is no surprise that research papers discussing these 'treatments' reveal a shocking lack of care towards the autistic children involved. For example, one paper from 1974 promotes the use of 'painful electric shocks' to force autistic children into compliance. In addition, the paper regularly compares autistic children with 'normal children'. When discussing a treatment designed to address self-harm, the author confesses: 'Incidentally, it would have been quite possible for us to have killed Greg through this treatment.'[2]

The seeming indifference the paper evinces towards the autistic children involved, and to the fact that being forced to comply might damage their quality of life, normalises a process of dehumanisation. This paper was published almost fifty years ago, and yet it seems little has changed.

Ableism is nothing new. Its roots in colonial constructions of whiteness and theories of eugenics stretch back over a hundred years. Francis Galton, who coined the term 'eugenics' in 1883, was primarily concerned with creating what he deemed 'an improved race of humans' that would be rid of anything that 'impaired' the population mentally and physically. Many American eugenicists asserted that certain groups of people (determined by race, class, and disability) were 'unfit' or 'feebleminded', and that procreation with them would hinder the future of the white elites.

This combination of racism and ableism is what led to the rise of many anti-miscegenation laws that banned marriage or sexual relations between interracial couples, and to widespread sterilisation campaigns around the world. Unfortunately, these two systems of oppression – racism and ableism – continue to be interlinked, working in tandem to maintain an unjust social hierarchy. The relationship between the two might help explain why, for example, black people in the UK are four times as likely to be detained under the Mental Health Act as white people.[3] This perhaps stems from racist assumptions about which patients pose the greatest 'threat' to others, or perhaps from the reduced support and lack of access to formal diagnosis for people of colour. It means that, by the time they interact with health care systems, they are already in crisis. Given the large number of neurodivergent people who suffer from mental health difficulties, it is a fair assumption that many of those individuals detained will be neurodivergent (whether or not they have received a diagnosis).

Ableism, then, has been used for some time as a means of segregating those deemed 'deviants' from normal society. In 1952, the first edition of the *Diagnostic and Statistical Manual of Mental Disorders* included homosexuality under 'sociopathic personality disturbance', as well as a subcategory titled 'sexual deviant', which included transvestism and transsexuality. While homosexuality is no longer officially considered a psychiatric condition, this pathologisation of sexual identity demonstrates the power with which ableism is wielded to medicalise and discriminate against those who live their lives in a certain way, as well as emphasising how this treatment of groups can fluctuate over time.

Unfortunately, the overlap between the pathologisation of neurodivergence and that of 'deviant' sexuality and gender has a long history. This is best understood through the work of Ole Ivar Løvaas. Løvaas is commonly known in autism circles as the founder of the controversial applied behaviour analysis (ABA). Løvaas is quoted as saying that he hoped to use the therapy to make autistic people 'normal'.[4] Many autistic people who have been through ABA have reported it as a harrowing experience, much akin to abuse. Academics have stated that there are ethical concerns with ABA, and there is evidence that exposure to it can cause PTSD symptoms. There is a growing movement around the desire to ban it, because people believe it punishes autistic people for not being able to fit into societal norms. There is also continued controversy around the decision of ABA therapists to use or condone treatments such as electric shock therapy.

Løvaas was also involved in the creation of the Feminine Boy Project of the 1970s, which sought to identify 'interventions' for the gender identities and behaviours of young people that were believed to be 'in need of fixing'. This is known today as gay and trans 'conversion therapy'. Løvaas saw non-conforming sexual and gender identities as disabling psychiatric conditions. Entrenched ableism and a desire to rid young people of these behaviours led directly to the violence and discrimination that followed.

Margaret Gibson and Patty Douglas explain the malice at the heart of this project using Lauren Berlant's theory of 'cruel optimism'. Cruel optimism occurs when something you desire becomes a hindrance to your well-being. Gibson and Douglas argue that Løvaas offered behavioural therapy as a sort of 'holy grail', on the basis that those diagnosed with autism or non-normative gender behaviours from a young age were hopeless cases who had not successfully taken to any other type of therapy or treatment. Løvaas marketed himself as the answer parents had been looking for – a source of optimism for those who had felt theirs had been depleted.

As Gibson and Douglas observe,

> The cruelty lies in how the measurements and interventions of this 'optimism' dehumanize, coerce, regulate, and do bodily violence to those deemed in need of a 'cure,' while recruiting and training others (teachers, parents, community members) to extend this pathologization, even at a cost to themselves.[5]

Løvaas's ABA therapy for 'disturbed' autistic children involved the heavy use of positive reinforcements, both verbal ('Good boy!') and physical, in the form of hugs. These were combined with negative reinforcements, which included 'slaps, electric shocks, and reprimands for undesired/autistic behaviours such as flapping hands, rocking, banging body parts against objects, climbing on furniture, not coming to the experimenter when asked, not hugging the experimenter, or averting their gaze'.[6]

While his treatments for the Feminine Boy Project were not as violent, they did include requiring parents to ignore their child when they engaged in an 'undesired' behaviour such as picking a feminine toy, and they gave licence to parents to create their own home training programmes 'that could include striking the child'.[7]

What Gibson and Douglas highlight through their dissection of Løvaas's work is how a sense of hopelessness was crucial to his project. Løvaas, who in his own words described some autistic test subjects as 'indistinguishable from their *normal* friends' after treatment, was committed to the narrative that autistic and gender-nonconforming children were in dire need of fixing.[8] This hopelessness is what, for him, justified violent treatment that was – and remains – unethical.

This imperative to do whatever it takes to try to 'cure' autistic behaviour is no less common now. As parents and researchers do everything they can to restore 'normal functioning' in autistic people, an intense pathologisation of neurodivergence continues. In recent years this search for a cure has led parents to administer substances like chlorine dioxide (similar to bleach) orally, in baths and through enemas, known in the community under the humble title of 'Miracle Mineral Solution'.[9] As recently as 2023, a mother with 109,000 followers on TikTok calls herself a 'Self-Healing Autism Mom'. While in her TikTok bio she says, 'I'm not a doctor, I don't give medical advice', she has nonetheless gained popularity for sharing a 'detox bath tutorial' that she claims helps autistic children with speech delays to begin speaking, stops repetitive stimming, and puts an end to food aversion (often caused by tactile or olfactory experiences).[10] She claims that the bath helps to 'pull out heavy metals from [children's] little bodies' as she believes heavy metals to be the cause for developmental disabilities. While a comment from another user states that the mother is not making any money from such tips, she does in fact sell a 'Detox Guide' for children who are autistic or have ADHD, which costs almost $50.[11]

In the early 2000s, another proposal for curing autism was found in churches. News broke in 2003 that an autistic child had been killed during an 'exorcism' carried out in an attempt to save the boy from what the community believed to be 'demonic possession'.[12] Of course, this was not the first or last time that religion was responsible for controversial opinions on the existence of autism. 'Why did god give me an autistic child?' is a popular Google search; and one blog from the parent of an autistic child reports that their pastor asked whether their child's autism might be the result of 'unconfessed sins'.[13]

With only a century's worth of research into autism, incredibly large amounts of money and time have been spent to try and find a cure; but no cure has been found. Perhaps it is time to cease this relentless effort, and instead turn to research that focuses on providing a better quality of life. If the neurodiversity campaign wants to tackle the ableism that fuels so much of the abuse faced by neurodivergent people, then it must continue to refute the claim that being autistic (or otherwise neurodivergent) is not a valid, worthwhile way of existing in the world. It must fight against any instance of dehumanisation and tackle this idea of 'hopelessness' that still pervades society's opinion of autistic and/or disabled people today. It is essential to any sort of success that we curb the narratives that deny autistic and neurodivergent people their humanity.

Making the Connection

Not all neurodivergent people are disabled, but many are. This means that many neurodivergent people spend their lives feeling that the world around them is inaccessible, or they spend countless hours fighting for basic accommodations that will enable them to live their lives. Beyond having to fight simply to have space made for them to exist, many suffer from the world's hostility towards disabled people. They are faced with discrimination, abuse, and exclusion, and the extent of their mistreatment is often determined by their other markers of identity.

For this reason, if the neurodiversity campaign seeks to combat the instances of oppression with which so many neurodivergent people must grapple, it must also confront the other systemic discrimination they face as a result of their intersecting identities. In order to understand and confront these complex systems of power, it is necessary for the neurodiversity campaign to consider and incorporate the work of those organising in disability justice spaces.

Many of the neurodiversity campaign's successes can be credited to the work of activists from the disability rights and autism rights camp. Jim Sinclair's seminal 2012 work, 'Don't Mourn for Us', was one of the first pieces that explicitly rejected the idea of a cure for autism – a position that now represents a central part of neurodiversity.[14] Sinclair was also responsible for Autreat, an annual conference run by and for autistic adults which provided one of the first physical spaces in which autistic people could build a community around their shared experiences.

Despite these successes, there have been numerous claims that disability rights as a wider movement has not successfully accounted for further marginalised disabled people, such as those who also face oppression because of their race, class, gender or other characteristics.[15] While the disability rights movement has fought hard for long-overdue legal rights and pushed for the empowerment of disabled people, many felt that the movement failed to interrogate the systems permeated by ableism that put multiply marginalised disabled people at risk – systems like prisons, the police, capitalism, and so on.

Patty Berne outlined this failure to consider wider systems by explaining that while the disability rights movement was a step forward for disabled people, it 'simultaneously invisibilized the lives of people who live at intersecting junctures of oppression'.[16]

If neurodiversity is to be successful, it must account for the intersecting identities that exist within society and the ways in which each social identity determines the treatment a neurodivergent person receives. Only by this means will it gain a full understanding of the various levels of discrimination and oppression experienced by neurodivergent people, and what we can do to combat them.

⊷

The original Disability Justice Collective was formed in 2005 in response to these failings of the disability rights movement. It began as the work of queer, disabled women of colour Patty Berne, Mia Mingus, and Stacy Milbern, before they invited Leroy Moore, Eli Clare, and Sebastian Margeret to join. Working as writers, organisers, and educators, the group formed the movement as a vehicle to demand collective liberation. A definition of Disability Justice reads:

> Disability Justice was built because the Disability Rights Movement and Disability Studies do not inherently centralize the needs and experiences of folks experiencing intersectional oppression, such as disabled people of color, immigrants with disabilities, queers with disabilities, trans and gender non-conforming people with disabilities, people with disabilities who are houseless, people with disabilities who are incarcerated, people with disabilities who have had their ancestral lands stolen, amongst others.[17]

Sins Invalid, a disability justice–based performance project founded by Patty Berne and others, developed the following ten principles of disability justice:

1. Intersectionality
2. Leadership of Those Most Impacted
3. Anti-Capitalist Politics
4. Commitment to Cross-Movement Organizing
5. Recognizing Wholeness

6. Sustainability
7. Commitment to Cross-Disability Solidarity
8. Interdependence
9. Collective Access
10. Collective Liberation[18]

Disability Justice makes the demand for liberation, not assimilation. It promotes the idea that we must not strive to fit disabled people into a world that already does not value them or their lives. By highlighting how ableism is linked to other forms of oppression, the movement demands that we make use of cross-movement solidarity to take these systems apart and rebuild them, so that we can guarantee access to justice for all, no longer treating disability as a singular, one-sided issue.

Mia Mingus describes part of this process as 'moving beyond access'. Rather than fighting solely for disabled people to be given the same rights as everyone else, we tear things down and begin again, to create instead a world where inaccessibility could not even exist. She describes that while accessibility is of course vital to every disabled person's life, there is more to be done to combat isolation, to eliminate ableism and the way it infiltrates our cultures, and to combat what she calls the 'myth of independence'.[19]

She argues that our world – especially the Western world, where hyper-individualism is rampant – promotes an ideal of the 'independent individual' who needs nothing from anyone and can live their life successfully and happily without the input or support of others. Mingus argues that this is a false-hood, that we are all dependent on others in ways we do not even consider. Who made your clothes? Who harvested your vegetables? Who built your home?

This myth of independence also carries an ableist undercur-rent. Speaking of Mingus's work in this area, Mariame Kaba notes:

> That's what Mia says all the time: the notion that we suppos-edly are not interdependent on each other can only exist in an ableist world. Because if you have any sort of disability, you desperately need a relationship with other people – you can't be on your own or you will die. You have to recognize the interdependence, or build interdependence. You don't have a choice.[20]

Mingus's notion of 'interdependence' describes the belief that we do need each other, every one of us, and that we would benefit from admitting this and building it into our cultures and our systems. We are dependent on one another, and we should both work towards removing the shame that can arise from this need for connection and help, as well as stop posi-tioning independence as a source of achievement. No one's success is their own.

Disability justice informs the work of organisers who already interrogate our harmful systems, such as Lydia X. Z. Brown, an autistic attorney and disability justice advocate.[21] Brown's work as a lawyer for disabled people of colour has exposed the complex mistreatment faced by some of the most marginalised members of society and formed their belief that 'we can't address disability without addressing race.'[22]

In their essay of the same name, they highlight a report from UCLA's Civil Rights Project, which finds that many US school districts are not only failing to identify disabled students who might benefit from additional support, but also that students of colour are more likely to attend schools in districts where this lack of identification is more prevalent.[23] This leaves them without support at disproportionate rates.

The report also demonstrates that, while disabled students in general face much higher rates of out-of-school suspensions than their non-disabled peers, the impact on disabled students of colour is even higher. This directly corresponds with Lydia's experience of defending some of the most marginalised students against excessive policing.

Lydia further highlights the increased criminalisation of disabled people of colour – something that is reflected in statistical evidence going far beyond the schooling environment. In the United States, reports have found that half of all people killed by police officers are disabled, and that by the age of twenty-eight more than half of disabled African-Americans have been arrested – double the number reported for white disabled Americans.[24]

A recent case that emphasises the extent of this penalisation is that of Neli Latson, a black autistic teen who was sitting outside the library on one of his regular walks when he was arrested after a stranger called the police to report him as a 'suspicious male, possibly in possession of a gun'. He did not have a gun, but he was sentenced to ten years in prison – much of which he spent in solitary confinement, in one instance for almost a year.[25]

These individuals are subject to the workings of racist, ableist systems that control the whole of their lives based on a few instances of bias. Lydia's work demonstrates that facing unjust, punitive action more often than their white, non-disabled peers puts them at risk of harsher consequences for actions that might otherwise have been overlooked. By failing to interrogate the systems that enforce these biased actions, we are curbing the trajectories of people's lives.

These are just some examples picked from countless others that showcase the impact of the discriminatory systems that continuously harm neurodivergent and disabled people of colour. They are depressing statistics that relate to the carceral mindset in the West, which instinctively seeks to punish in every instance, without considering whether we are collectively failing the people in question.

Many of the students referenced in the UCLA report mentioned above will be neurodivergent – indeed, the report confirms this in mentioning students with ADHD. The neuro-diversity campaign should strongly favour interrogating the racist undertones of a system that disproportionately harms students of colour. By linking the neurodiversity campaign with the aims of disability justice, we can call for systemic discrimination to be effectively addressed – demanding the investigation of intersectional inequities that exist between neurodivergent people, and a response to it. In this instance, the linking of the neurodiversity campaign with the work of disability justice could use the findings of this report to consider what can be done differently to identify *all* students who need extra support. By addressing the racial inequity within the system, we could ensure that additional services are adequate for every student's mental and behavioural needs.

In the context of racial inequity, connecting the work of the neurodiversity campaign with that of disability justice might look like considering the ways that families of colour are forced to survive multiple forms of oppression, and how this impacts the way that they advocate for their neurodivergent family members.

This is something that autistic advocates Tiffany (@fidgets. and.fries on Instagram) and TJ (@nigh.functioning.autism) discuss frequently on their platforms. As neurodivergent people who are also parents of neurodivergent children, they explore the nuances of facing their circumstances while also dealing with violent, racist systems.

They ask that people consider the fact that there are families that have neurodivergent children with high support needs who have been forced to turn to controversial treatments like ABA because they have no access to alternative care services.

TJ, in particular, highlights the concept of 'masking', a well-known phenomenon in which autistic people suppress their spontaneous behaviour because they know that it will be received negatively, and in the worst cases put them at risk of bullying or mistreatment. TJ notes that, while she understands that masking is associated with poor mental health, she is forced to warn her children that, because of how the world reacts to them as people of colour, they will sometimes be required to mask in order to ensure their safety. It is a privilege that white, especially middle-class autistic people like me can act with more agency and not be penalised for the choice not to mask.

An understanding of the racial disparities faced by families with disabled children requires us to recognise that they may agree with those advocates who call for an end to therapies like ABA, or the expectation for neurodivergent people to mask. But they are also grappling with the fact that they must prepare their child for a world that is aggressively hostile to them because of their intersecting identities. The oppression they face cannot be met with apathy, or some expressions of it prioritised over others. The type of discrimination they face is formed by every facet of their identity. If the neurodiversity campaign is to be successful, it must integrate this perspective.

As an autistic lesbian, I am keenly aware of the growing conversation around neurodivergence and the breakdown of cisheteronormativity. Recent studies suggest that transgender and gender-diverse people are between three and six times as likely as cisgender adults to be diagnosed as autistic.[26] While the exact figure has yet to be determined for sexuality, most sources suggest that autistic people are more likely to identify as non-heterosexual.[27] Following these studies and others like them, a link between neurodivergence and rejection of sexual and gender norms seems clear.

While I refuse to pathologise these findings, since they do not represent a problem to be solved, it is possible that they suggest that, having already transgressed the boundaries of neuro-conformity, neurodivergent people find it easier to confront other social norms, or are simply more likely to break more than one norm at a time.

Whatever the basis of these tendencies, what is most important is the need to address the increased risk of discrimination that arises from being both neurodivergent and queer.[28] As sexuality- and gender-related hate crimes continue around the world, particularly in the UK and the United States, many queer people worry for their safety – especially those already at a higher risk of discrimination due to their neurodivergence. Considering these issues while keeping the framework of disability justice in mind, it becomes clear that fighting for the rights of neurodivergent people also means fighting for the rights of LGBTQIA2S+ people.[29]

A recent example of this merging of ableism with other types of oppression is Georgia's new anti-trans law, signed by the American state's governor in March 2023. SB 140, a bill created to criminalise various types of gender-affirming care, includes a clause stating that gender dysphoria 'is often comorbid with other mental health and developmental conditions, including autism spectrum disorder'.[30] The bill weaponises autism to justify control over trans and gender non-conforming people, preventing access to gender-affirming care that is in many cases life-saving.

It demonstrates how ableism and transphobia/cissexism gain more power when used in tandem against anyone whose existence falls outside dominant, socialised norms. It dictates that those autistic people whose experience of gender identity goes beyond the established binary should not be trusted to have enough insight to decide whether or not they want to make decisions about their own bodies.

This bill, an example of institutional violence, demonstrates how much more harm can be done when oppressive systems combine multiple forms of power, subjugating larger groups of marginalised people, and in many cases pathologising them for representing a perceived threat to cisheteronormativity or other pervasive systems.[31]

Alongside the increased risk of discrimination faced by neuro-divergent queer people, there is growing concern around their treatment in research spaces. The application of pathological language to sexuality and gender imposes an additional layer of 'othering' on people who are already medicalised because of their neurotype. One study of this phenomenon found a significant amount of cisgenderism in case studies of autistic trans people, with one paper even referring to a cisgender heterosexual identity as a 'healthy' one, pathologising all other identities.[32] Replete with the misgendering of the individuals and the use of culturally constructed ideas about how each gender should behave, the case studies were completed by authors whose understanding of gender was bio-essentialist and contributed to the direct pathologisation of their neuro-divergent subjects – determining that they were 'abnormal' in more ways than one.

Nick Walker has much to teach us about what happens when we combine liberatory theories of queerness and neurodiversity. Having written extensively on what she calls the 'neurodiversity paradigm', Nick is a queer, transgender, autistic writer who is one of the individuals credited with the term 'neuroqueer'. Describing it as something she always envisioned as 'a verb first, and an adjective second', she explains that it was conceived to describe 'the practice of queering (subverting, defying, disrupting, liberating oneself from) neuronormativity and heteronormativity simultaneously'.[33]

Breaking free from predetermined, limiting social norms, neuroqueering works to interrogate the ways in which, while growing up, we are bound by a cluster of socially constructed roles and habits, and dissuaded from questioning their nature or origin. It offers the opportunity to exist outside what-ever box we were forced into at birth. The key for me is the emphasis on linking one liberatory practice with another, something that I believe is essential for neurodiversity to achieve its aims. Walker writes, 'I couldn't truly liberate myself from heteronormativity without also liberating myself from neuronormativity, and I couldn't truly liberate myself from neuronormativity without also liberating myself from heteronormativity.'[34]

Walker's exposure of the interconnectedness of these two concepts leads me to my final point. Each individual's experience of neurodivergence is likely to be heavily conditioned by their other experiences of the world – experiences determined by race, gender, sexuality, class, other disabilities, and much else. This means that, if we truly want to create safer, better lives for neurodivergent people, we must face up to the other systems that determine their quality of life and potentially cause them harm.

Disability justice is a movement that allows us to examine the many structures and systems that abuse and harm marginalised individuals. It allows us to consider how these systems are interwoven, and work in parallel to create stronger forces of subjugation and silencing. When combined with the work of the neurodiversity movement, I believe it helps us to calculate the additional risks faced by neurodivergent people with multiple marginalised aspects of their identity. It can motivate us to work towards pulling down discriminatory structures, abolishing the systems that cause harm and suffering to so many across the globe, and help us consider what we might want to build in their place, and what it might look like to build something that takes everyone's needs and experiences into account.

Linking the neurodiversity campaign to a larger politics of liberation creates a broader network against injustice. Ridding our society of the punishing systems that affect neurodivergent people not only benefit neurodivergent people themselves, but also everyone else. Taking down one oppressive system will

require taking down the others as well; no marginalised group
will be truly liberated until everyone is.

Today it is possible to identify how ableist mindsets shape
the lives of disabled people by looking at cases like the
treatment of children in Doncaster care homes. One child,
Ruby, is autistic, and has epilepsy and learning difficulties.
She is reported as having suffered at the hands of many of
the care staff, being dragged across the floor and punished
with enforced sensory overload. In private messages, staff
admit to having hit her.[35]

By subscribing to a status quo that sees those outside
constructed norms as 'deficient', we have given ourselves
the power to decide who is and is not to be considered human.
Through this kind of ideology, a social hierarchy is perpetuated
that places groups of people at risk of all manner of discrimination, violence, mistreatment, and abuse. Historically, this has
been applied to the most marginalised people in our societies,
who are punished for no other reason than being one way
rather than another.

This focus on deficiency is particularly pointed in the case
of autism. As Robert Chapman and Havi Carel point out,
'autism is widely taken to be at odds – to varying extents –
with both well-being and flourishing, and hence incompat-
ible with both objective and subjective conceptions of the
good life'.[36] This widespread assumption that autistic people
are unable to thrive because they are in some way deficient
leads to a reluctance to treat autistic people as human. And

the same is true for any marginalised group that is thought
to deviate from social norms, in some way 'threatening' the
dominant social order.

It is easy to overlook the unjust treatment of a group
of people if you consider them to be less than human, in
some way undeserving of, or incapable of achieving, a happy,
'good' life. Chapman and Carel suggest that the dominant,
pathologising view of autism might mean that 'we have been
rendered ignorant of the possibility of distinctly autistic
forms of thriving in certain ways due to interlocking biases,
stigma, and prejudice'.[37] Not only do I believe this to be true;
I also believe that it can be applied far beyond autism, and
contributes heavily to the way in which ableism functions
in our world.

The inaccessibility of society is often overlooked by non-
disabled people. How many times in the past month have you
socialised in a pub, restaurant, or social space that would be
inaccessible to those in a wheelchair, those who cannot stand
for long periods of time, or those who struggle with sensory
overload in environments with lots of loud talking? How
about the spaces where you exercise, work, or live? If you take
a minute to consider their architecture and the experience of
being inside them, who do they exclude?

Disabled people are often forgotten about, or simply
ignored. Ableism functions in such a way as to force them
into a separate class, different and deficient in some way
from everyone else. The extent of the mistreatment they
face is determined by many other factors, as I have described,

which means that many face multiple forms of oppression throughout their lives.

Neurodivergent and/or disabled people belong in this world just as much as anyone else. They do not deserve to live in a world that is inaccessible, ableist, and often downright violent towards them. Each person has a life that is theirs to live.

4
NEURODIVERSITY, WORK, AND POVERTY

I am part of a very small percentage of employed autistic people. With varying levels of success, I have had jobs since I was sixteen – the first being at Papa John's, which taught me that people take their pizza seriously.

Disclosing my autism diagnosis to employers has been risky, and sometimes more trouble than it's worth. One manager, after my disclosure a month into employment, switched the tone in which he spoke to me to one you might use in conversation with young children. He began ending each shift we did together by giving me a high five and assuring me that I had done a good job. This treatment was not meted out to my colleagues – nor had he used it with me before I had told him I was autistic.

The most recent UK figures indicate that autistic people and people with learning disabilities face a higher rate of unemployment than any other group of disabled individuals. They show that just 21.7 per cent of autistic people and 5.1 per cent of people with a learning disability are in any type of employment.[1] These numbers vary around the world, but generally remain low. In Australia it is estimated that 40 per cent of autistic people are employed.[2] In China this number stands at less than 10 per cent.[3] Data from many other parts of the world are scarce, reflecting the lack of resources needed for collecting data about neurodivergent people. Neurodivergent people are certainly not the only marginalised group who struggle to access stable, well-paid employment; but I have no doubt that this problem undermines the independence and livelihoods of many neurodivergent adults.

I do not believe that the core aim of the politics of a fairer understanding of neurodiversity is to make neurodivergent people more productive under capitalism. I do not believe that our goal should be to venture down a path on which the goal is to make everyone capable of labouring, or that we should expose as many people as possible to capitalist exploitation. I do not believe that a human life is rendered worthwhile simply by virtue of its relation to the means of production, or that having a job makes a person any more worthy of a good life than anyone else.

Rather I believe that those who are unable to work, for whatever reason, deserve access to the same resources that provide a good quality of life enjoyed by everyone else. Every single person on earth has the potential to face periods of temporary or permanent unemployment – this is an enduring truth, and I do not believe that it renders any of us deserving of mistreatment, discrimination, or hardship. We cannot improve the lives of neurodivergent people until we improve their material conditions, and for the moment this involves addressing the problems with employment, since this is one dimension of the societal exclusion that puts disabled people at risk of living in poverty.

Work under capitalism, in short, is not great. But being unable to work under capitalism is even worse. Life is made extremely difficult for anyone unable to work because of the way our society is organised, and this has dire consequences for many neurodivergent people.

As Amelia Horgan discusses in her book *Lost in Work*, work is becoming increasingly dismal as the gap between the rich and the poor continues to widen all over the world. But beyond this, 'the world outside of work is one of punitive benefit sanctions and moral condemnation.'[4] Being dependent on the welfare state is becoming progressively more difficult as continual benefit cuts, crumbling public services, worsening stigma, and global crises rage on.

Steep rates of unemployment seem to be consistent across the diagnoses that fall under the umbrella of neurodiversity. One UK study showed that there was a '50% difference in employment rates between ADHD and control groups'.[5] Meanwhile, for those with learning disabilities the employment rate has continued to drop over the years. I have failed a large number of job interviews myself, including a six-hour trial shift as a dishwasher for a shop that never even bothered to call me and let me know I had not got the job. After finishing my master's degree, I completed forty-three job applications before receiving an internship.

The reason these startling statistics matter is that they are connected to a wider state of inequality that affects disabled people disproportionately. As I write this, people in the UK face a cost-of-living crisis in which inflation has reached over 10 per cent. This crisis is expected to affect disabled people, and therefore many neurodivergent people, at an astounding rate. The newest research suggests that, on average, disabled households now need an additional £975 a month to maintain the same standard of living as non-disabled households. These additional costs often caused by an increased need for essential services like heating and disability equipment.[6] Due to these additional costs, studies in the UK estimate that 28 per cent of those living in poverty are disabled (3.9 million), while a further 20 per cent of those in poverty live in a household with a disabled person (2.7 million).[7] This clearly demonstrates that disabled people's material conditions have not been a priority for the British state, which has allowed them to be overlooked.

This association between disability and poverty is not limited to the UK. While the amount of data collected varies from country to country, one study using internationally comparable results from Guatemala, India, and Cameroon found that, across all three countries, disabled people faced higher levels of poverty.[8]

What Should Be Done?

It is clear that the systems under which we now operate are not working; but knowing what needs to be changed can be difficult.

A redistribution of wealth and resources should remain our core goal, and some ideas that would offer widespread benefits include the following.

Improving working conditions
In 2016, the National Autistic Society ran a study which found that 48 per cent of employed autistic people reported experiencing bullying or harassment in the workplace.[9] This kind of discrimination is one of the driving forces behind neurodivergent peoples' decision not to disclose their diagnoses at work, as well as the struggle they face in finding employment at all.[10] The social acceptance that would likely come with an understanding of neurodiversity and a shift in societal attitudes would hopefully aid the creation of safer workplace environments.

Through increasing social acceptance and accommodation, companies might begin to make it easier for people to disclose their diagnosis. However, it is important to note that many accommodations that would benefit neurodivergent people – as I will discuss below – would also benefit all workers. The ultimate goal should be to work closely with unions, taking account of employees' needs to provide accessibility for all workers regardless of their diagnosis.

There are many barriers to employment for neurodivergent people, and I cannot possibly capture the needs of every single individual here. I will instead try to list some of the issues that could be tackled.

Creating a better sensory environment
This includes building sensory maps such as those used in public spaces like the British Museum; creating spaces for quiet working or allowing the use of headphones; building offices with as much natural light as possible, and avoiding the use of harsh artificial lighting.[11] This approach can be applied far beyond the realm of work environments, considering the inaccessibility of many other spaces, both public and private. What would it mean to consider the experience of neurodivergent people on public transport, on an average street, at hospital, or in their own homes? What does it mean to prioritise accessibility in architectural design? In 2022, the British Standards Institution released its first-ever building design standard for sensory and neurological needs, demonstrating the potential for further work in this area.[12]

Creating accessible physical and digital spaces
This includes working with accessibility auditors and consultancies to address issues for disabled people. For example, could a wheelchair user work from your office? Can someone who uses a screen reader use your internal communications system? How would your company accommodate a Deaf person?

Increasing understanding and acceptance
This includes cracking down on workplace discrimination and ableism; providing workplace neurodiversity training (from neurodivergent professionals – be wary of hiring those who

will perpetuate ableist myths); not patronising neurodivergent people or treating them as a novelty in the workplace.

Communication

Vague directions or feedback and unclear communication should be avoided. Non-verbal communication and indirect verbal communication should be reduced. Verbal communication should be clear and concise, and thought should be given to how to accommodate workers who use assistive technologies such as augmentative and alternative communication devices. Accommodation should also be made for the use of non-verbal systems such as Stickman Communications.[13] Sign-language courses should be provided for employees, and interviews offered in various formats: relaxed, informal conversation, sharing of interview questions in advance, the offer of multiple meetings to get to know the interviewee, instead of a single all-or-nothing interview.

Flexibility

Workers should be offered the opportunity to work from home or engage in hybrid working, if possible, and offered flexible working hours. I appreciate the fact that my colleagues allow me to reschedule meetings if I am feeling socially overwhelmed or fatigued, and that they do not object if I ask them to give me the details of a task over email rather than via a video call. I am also lucky enough to have the option of working from home most of the time. If I were forced into the office environment regularly, it is unlikely I would perform well, because I would struggle to cope with the relentless sensory overload. Having this level of work flexibility would also benefit those who have to care for neurodivergent family or friends.

Stability

The increasing rates of zero-hour contracts, a growing gig economy, and unstable employment have a negative impact on everyone. But this kind of instability and constant change is particularly difficult for neurodivergent people. Offering more stable working conditions will benefit everyone, especially neurodivergent people.

Learning

Most employers have very little understanding of what it might entail to have more neurodivergent people in work. Remedying this will require an openness to confronting previously held beliefs about disability and preconceived ideas of what a 'good worker' might look like. Employers may benefit from the work of charities like MENCAP, who produce reports such as *Access All Areas* that explore the opening up of work and apprenticeships for people with learning disabilities.

Listening

As the fields of neurodiversity studies and disability studies continue to grow, an ever-increasing amount of work is required in collecting the experiences of neurodivergent and disabled people to determine what accommodations might bring about real change. I believe articles like Ravi Malhotra's and Jacqueline Moizer's 'Crip Time, Law and the Duty to Accommodate: Toward a Legal-Materialist Understanding of the Lives of Workers with Disabilities' are worth consulting.[14] Carried out in Canada, the project explores the idea of 'crip time' – the idea that, due to the fact that things such as accessible transportation or attendant services can often be late, if delivered at all, disabled people experience time in a different way to non-disabled people – as a factor in understanding best practices for employing disabled people using their lived experience.

A study of German autistic adults with 'above-average' education showed that, despite their education, an 'alarmingly large unemployment gap' remained between them and their non-autistic counterparts, demonstrating that the biggest factor keeping neurodivergent people out of the labour market is the labour market itself.[15]

The world of work is currently hostile towards neurodivergent people; but it is also not ideal for most other people. Changing the nature of work by working closely with unions and organisers who understand what solutions would best serve all workers would promote a general improvement in standards of working. More specifically, by using the research around neurodivergent people at work, we can achieve an understanding of what accommodations might be most beneficial in closing the employment gap.

Accommodations should be freely given to anyone who asks, without any requirement of proof of diagnosis or other explanation. They should transform what working is like for everyone, so that anyone who does need accommodations can access them without fear of repercussions or intrusive questioning.

Changing Our Mindsets

It is not the aim of neurodiversity to get neurodivergent people into work. Neurodiversity in its truest form is anti-capitalist. It rejects the idea that each of us is only as worthy as what we produce – that we should be valued by how much we labour, and how much we accumulate in a world driven by overconsumption.

One of capitalism's most successful achievements in the Western world is its move towards individualism. We have been told that we should see each other only as competitors for the jobs we want; we are taught that it is a worthwhile practice to measure ourselves against one another in the race to own as much as possible. Whether it is houses, cars, or clothes – the more you have, and the more expensive what you have is, the more successful you are deemed to be under capitalism. As a young autistic person trying to fit in by mimicking the behaviours of classmates, I understood the perceived social currency of the most desired items at each moment, whether it was a Blackberry phone or the latest handbag.

But this individualistic mindset has offered us little in return. We are destroying our planet, suffering from ever-increasing inequality, and burning out mentally and physically from a 'hustle' culture that benefits only those privileged by their socioeconomic status. This mindset is completely antithetical to the care we must take to create a world where all are valued. We must therefore reject the penchant for self-interest and the desire for profits above everything else.

This individualism has brought up important questions in neurodiversity around the possibility of being in 'community' with people simply because you share an identity characteristic (such as being autistic). Arguments have been made that, as capitalism sinks its teeth into neurodiversity, it is creating a space in which a neurodivergent identity is coming to constitute a form of social capital. This may be through the work of social media 'influencers', or those who have weaponised neurodivergence in order to argue that they might not enjoy other forms of socioeconomic privilege. This process of making neurodivergence 'marketable' can lead to a form of hyper-individualism that rejects the true tenets of neurodiversity and fails to advocate for those who have the least proximity to power, or whose politics reject the imperatives of capital.

Neurodiversity should disavow the quest for endless economic growth at the expense of the many, as well as the betrayal of those most at risk in the pursuit of capital gain. Neurodiversity demands that we forbid the social exclusion of those unable to participate in work, and that we rethink our politics – moving from a politics of self-interest to one of care and solidarity.

Neurodivergent people must not be viewed as puppets for

profit. Our entry into the workplace must not be examined for its potential to increase gains for shareholders. We should be included as part of the workplace as ourselves, no more or less valuable than any other worker.

Avoiding this fetishistic approach to neurodivergent people might rescue us from what Robert Chapman calls 'Neoliberal Neurodiversity', used to 'advance the outcomes of neurodivergent (usually autistic) people without fundamentally challenging neoliberalism or capitalism more broadly'.[16] This is particularly prominent in corporate environments. This kind of approach works only to put people into jobs to achieve company profits. A single-pronged approach to neurodiversity, it simply ignores the other oppressive systems that limit neurodivergent people's daily lives.

Furthermore, there will always remain a number of neurodivergent people who are unable to work. Under our current system, life is made very difficult for these people, not just economically but also socially. As Horgan explains, 'under capitalism, work becomes the only avenue for self-development, respect, and fulfilment'.[17] This is because we have made it natural to tie work to our identities, shaping our lives around our work and what we accomplish in it.

This is why so many people who do not work face social exclusion or discrimination, being branded as 'benefit scroungers' or accused of not 'working hard enough'. The *Daily Telegraph* has gone so far as to produce a calculator that can 'reveal how much of your salary bankrolls the welfare state' – arguably inciting hatred and resentment towards disabled people unable to work because of how much they 'cost'.[18]

Frances Ryan explores the extent of this demonisation in the case of disabled people, explaining that this scapegoating 'did not come about by accident', but was a direct result of the Conservative Party's austerity project. Creating a narrative that 'work-shy' benefit claimants were to blame for the staggering cuts to public services, this attack on a marginalised group not only enforced a status quo that harmed some of society's most vulnerable but was also factually incorrect. As Ryan reports, 'The Centre for Welfare Reform calculated in 2013 that disabled people would endure nine times the burden of cuts compared to the average citizen, with people with the most severe disabilities being hit a staggering nineteen times harder.'[19]

Neurodiversity urges us to rethink this position of contempt, to stop alienating the unemployed or deeming their lives to be any less valuable. Humans are not born to be profit-producers; once we understand this, we can begin reorganising society in a way that prioritises joy, respect, care, and acceptance. We cannot begin to reach any kind of equality until we cease to view work and material conditions as indices of human worth or the right to social participation.

The Benefit System

It is clear from the research on disability and poverty that the amount of financial assistance offered to disabled people is inadequate. It is essential that we take into account the additional costs borne by disabled people, an increase in benefits, and a reversal of the horrendous cuts made during the past decade. Working towards global wealth redistribution and improving the material conditions of those in need must be a central objective in the fight for liberation. Without taking measures to deal with financial inequality there is only so much we can achieve.

For those unable to work at all, benefit systems are harsh, and offer minimal support. After a decade of austerity and cuts, figures show that disabled people's benefits in the UK have shrunk by £5 billion, while 60 per cent of disability benefit claimants believe that the amount they receive is not enough to live on.[20] In the United States, those unable to work because of disability receive Social Security Disability Insurance. Due to the strictness of who is awarded this benefit, the Social Security Administration itself reports that this money is reserved for the most vulnerable people in society – the recipients being more than three times as likely to die within a year as non-recipients of the same age. It goes on to report that the payments are 'modest', and admits: 'At the beginning of 2019, Social Security paid an average monthly disability benefit of about $1,234 to all disabled workers. That is barely enough to keep a beneficiary above the 2018 poverty level ($12,140 annually).'[21]

In order to ensure financial security, the benefit system must offer increased economic support. The manner of its operation should also be scrutinised carefully. One issue is household means testing. At present, many neurodivergent people who claim Employment and Support Allowance in the UK because of their disability are forced to give it up when they choose to move in with partners. This puts individuals in a vulnerable position, rendering them financially dependent on non-disabled partners, and in some cases unable to leave abusive relationships because of financial difficulties. This kind of penalisation blocks disabled people from something as simple as cohabiting with partners, excluding them from traditional homemaking ideals and making it difficult for them to consider the idea of raising a family, should they wish to.

Part of what makes life so difficult for those seeking or in receipt of disability benefits is the derision and accusations of moral failure they encounter. In the UK, those unable to work are often condemned and subjected to a disdain that is reflected in the very systems that have been built to support such individuals. Right-wing newspapers like the *Daily Mail* have spent years printing stories about 'benefit cheats', leading to increased demonisation of those receiving benefits. Stories like 'Wheelchair-Bound Benefits Cheat Is Caught Falsely Claiming £17,000 in Disability Benefit by Photograph of Her Riding an ELEPHANT' perpetuate harmful rhetoric about who is 'really' disabled, and such stories put disabled people at risk of mistreatment.[22] Those who leave comments on articles like this declare that those on disability benefits should be intensely scrutinised, even suggesting the inclusion of mandatory passport checks and interrogations to determine how those on benefits have paid for a holiday.

The discrimination faced by disabled people accessing

benefits is so severe that, in the wake of welfare reform policies in the UK, the relevant UN Committee completed an
inquiry in 2016 into the maltreatment of disabled people that
found evidence of 'grave or systematic violations of rights of
people with disabilities'.[23] The report, which also found no
evidence of the supposed 'benefit fraud' that many disabled
people had been accused of, determined that the 'Fit for Work'
assessment – an evaluation now known as the Work Capability
Assessment, which is used to determine whether you are able
to work or if you're entitled to financial support – could not
efficiently account for the complex nature of many disabilities,
or for the support needed to perform a job.

This kind of systematic mistreatment is fuelled by a contempt
for unemployed disabled people that produces a public desire
to impose sanctions in the hope that they will act as punishment
for those who fail to work, or to work 'hard enough'. Until
these condescending attitudes are obliterated and a sufficient
social security system is put in place, neurodivergent people
will remain at risk of prejudice and injustice.[24]

Improving Public Services

As cultural attitudes continue to prioritise the individual above
all else, an increase in the privatisation of public services has
brought to light new problems for those that depend upon
them. As well as making up a large percentage of those accessing support from social care services, neurodivergent people
are often more likely to have co-occurring conditions that

require some form of medical care. This is especially true for autistic people, many of whom are prone to gastrointestinal disorders, and approximately 20 per cent of whom are likely to have epilepsy.[25]

I myself have spent many years in various types of NHS therapy for multiple psychiatric diagnoses that include bulimia, PTSD, and body dysmorphic disorder – not really a surprise when you consider how prevalent mental health difficulties are among autistic people. Alongside this, I have a cardiologist who I see to manage my tachycardia, and I have diagnoses of polycystic ovary syndrome and hypothyroidism, as well as having had juvenile osteoporosis as a child. I have also spent much time in physiotherapy to manage my hypermobility. I have spent a lot of time in doctors' offices over the years.

If we want to provide a good quality of life for neurodivergent people, then we must think about who owns and operates these public services. Those interested only in turning the largest possible profit are in no way concerned about service users and their experiences. We must focus on the quality of these systems, and not on how much money can be made for them, refusing the prioritisation of profit over human lives.

This means dedicating more public spending to these services and making them user-led and person-centred to ensure that they meet the needs of those who use them. Organisations such as Shaping Our Lives, who work to ensure that people have a say in the policies and services that support them, demonstrate the importance of listening to and valuing the input of service users.[26]

In many families with neurodivergent children, in which the parents are unable to work, a child reaching the end of school must face the crushing realisation that there is very little support left. This transition, difficult for any young person, is also marked by an absence of services that force many parents into unemployment in order to maintain care positions. A stark lack of services, research, or information available for neurodivergent adults leaves them and their families in a lurch.

Many parents of neurodivergent children, left with little to no support, and thrust into poverty by the costs of caring and a lack of free time, are accordingly living with high levels of stress. A 2020 report in the United States found that almost one-third of autistic children live in poverty, and that the material conditions of these families were also impacted by race and ethnicity. The same report found that 80 per cent of black families and 75 per cent of Hispanic families with autistic children faced material hardship, while for white families this number stood at 59 per cent.[27]

The pandemic exacerbated this situation for many carers. Reports showed that on average they lost twenty-five hours of the support they had previously received from public services or friends and family, while 72 per cent reported never having had any breaks from caring at all.[28]

Such statistics should not be used to make a value judgement about neurodivergent children or adults. They should instead alert us to the fact that we are failing to support these families properly, and that adequate care services should be a priority if we are committed to improving the lives of neurodivergent people and their families. They also demonstrate that, when research is conducted on how best to support these families, it must take into account other factors, such as race, and should consider how intersecting identities will affect material hardship.

The closure of many location-based services, such as day centres, in order to save money, has prompted a turn to community services like activity groups. While these may help to combat the isolation that many neurodivergent people feel, they do not provide adequate support to those with more complex needs, such as those who are multiply disabled and require additional accommodations, or who are kept out of certain activities by inaccessible public spaces.

Neurodivergent people and their families are in dire need of fully funded services that offer a diverse range of long-term support, and that are organised by and with people who respect and believe in the aims of the neurodiversity campaign. In 2020, the Health and Social Care Committee in the House of Commons estimated that £7 billion of additional funding was required to provide support to those who needed it.[29] With rising inflation, this number will only increase.

The Opportunity to Build Skills

I was lucky enough to have some university lecturers who were understanding and accommodating of my needs – a positive experience of learning that contrasted with what I had encountered during my final years at school. Whereas teachers at my secondary school made me feel ashamed of myself and my abysmal mental health, lecturers at university afforded me the space to be honest about what I found most difficult about the university learning environment. They listened, and they helped me seek out solutions where they existed.

However, there are many people who are kept out of university because of its inaccessibility – a fact that was brought up many times during the Covid-19 lockdowns. People who had previously been told they were unable to gain a place at university because departments could not provide virtual learning environments were rightly perturbed by the arrangements suddenly made to accommodate the needs of the wider student population. If these things were in fact possible, then why had they been deemed any less urgent when they were needed by a smaller number of students?

This lack of inclusion in education spaces reaches far beyond higher education. The most recent report from the National Autistic Society showed that, while most autistic children in the UK – 73 per cent – were in mainstream schools, only one in seven secondary schoolteachers had received any sort of training around working with autistic students.[30]

The inaccessibility of learning environments is a likely culprit for the fact that, in the UK, 42.7 per cent of non-disabled people had a degree as their highest qualification, while this was true for just 24.9 per cent of disabled people.[31] If we want neurodivergent people to work more, then we must give them the opportunity to develop the skills they need to do so. This not only means making universities accessible, but making all types of education accessible, as well as overcoming elitist stereotypes about which kind of education is most valuable.

Essential research is now being conducted into how post-secondary education institutions might recognise the inclusion of neurodivergent students and staff as an important issue, and begin implementing helpful changes.[32] It has been recognised that a system-wide approach is necessary if we are to begin to tackle these inequities, and that for the accommodations to be worthwhile neurodivergent people *must* be involved in informing their character.

This kind of research is valuable not only for universities and colleges, but also for schools, nurseries, apprenticeships, and any other type of education. If, as a society, we are to take seriously the idea of offering valuable education from cradle to coffin, all fields of education must be accessible.

As the neurodiversity campaign continues to grow in strength, we should aim to eliminate the stigma attached to neurodivergent students, in the hope that this will provide greater numbers of neurodivergent people with the opportunity to develop their chosen skills and achieve their aspirations.

Until we improve material conditions for neurodivergent people and their families, the cycle of inequality will continue. Until we stop viewing human life through the prism of work, inequality will remain or continue to worsen. There is no way around these truths.

I do not believe that, in order to be deserving of a good life, a person must be able to contribute to society in the form of labour. I do not believe that the determination of a person's 'productivity' under capitalism should indicate how worthy they are as a person, or how much access to life's necessities they should be afforded.

Neurodivergent people must be allowed to become active participants in the communities around them, regardless of their employment status. They must be factored into economic decisions, and not punished or socially condemned if they are unable to work. If they can work, that work must be accessible, stable, and well-paid – just as it should be for everyone else.

5
MOVING FORWARD

If neurodiversity as a project asks us to commit to not only fundamentally reorganising our societies but also completing changing cultural perceptions about cognitive experiences, disability, and the idea of a 'good' human life, then is it not fair to acknowledge its political nature? It is certainly far more than a euphemism for 'disability'.

The previous chapters have demonstrated that neurodivergent people are currently at risk of being crushed under false ideas of 'normality'. The binary oppositions that have been created in the service of hegemony and the status quo have been built within strict boundaries that alienate parts of the population. By assuming that there is only one 'correct' way of living and being, we have constructed a reality that is hostile to anyone whose experience places them outside these boundaries.

Neurodivergent people and their families are being failed every day – and we will continue to fail them until we begin factoring them into the creation of new systems.

We must resist the co-optation of the term 'neurodiversity'. Our understanding of this word must incorporate its political origins and capture the extent of what it hopes to achieve. It is not a mere buzzword, but a way of looking at the world. It has the power to change how we interact with, understand, and show up compassionately for one another. Many gifted writers have developed theories of neurodiversity, and of the kind of world they want to create with it. The possibilities are endless. At a time when the world feels so heavy, and often thick with disappointment, perhaps possibilities are our most valuable resource.

So, if we are dealing in the currency of possibility, what might we hope to change? The following ideas emerge from conversations I have had with other neurodivergent people and their loved ones – whispers of a world that may yet make space for them, too.

The Power of Language

It would be remiss of me not to mention the function of language in the architecture of the campaign. I am a white writer, writing in English from my home in Europe. While English is not the only language I speak, I must be conscious of the way that my whiteness and choice to write this book in English shapes my ability to capture the movement.

Like this book, much of the most popular writing on neuro-diversity is in English, and little of it has been translated. Is work on neurodiversity from other parts of the world being successfully translated? Can we assume that the lack of translation goes both ways?

Thinking about neurodiversity in the context of language and linguistics offers us a wealth of interesting questions to consider. How is neurodivergence being understood beyond the English-speaking world? Are there frameworks of knowledge and understanding that are not being successfully absorbed by the movement and given the consideration they deserve?

There is a duty for all of us to ensure that discussions of neurodiversity do not remain English-centric, or consider only the lives and experiences of those privileged by imperialist structures and geopolitical contexts. There is room to build on an internationalist approach to neurodiversity, one that is rich with the thinking and resistance that is present across the entire globe – using innovative approaches to understand and work with the breadth of people's sociocultural conditions.

This work has already begun, thanks to researchers such as Yulin Cheng, who asks what would be gained through the creation of global research partnerships, and what barriers might arise in the process of building them.[1] Presenting the work of activists such as Zemi Yenus in Ethiopia, organisations like Sangath in India, and Cheng's own advocacy efforts in Hong Kong, this research is vital to understanding both the strengths and the challenges that will be faced when we commit to improving neurodivergent people's lives around the world.

Much of this work pairs with more recent efforts to decolonise academic research, platforming the work of those who have been suffocated by white, Eurocentric institutions, and acknowledging thinking and experiences that have been dismissed in the past.

By surveying the diversity of language used in discussions of neurodivergence across the globe, we can understand the ways in which neurodivergence is culturally and linguistically constructed. What does it mean to be autistic in one country compared to another? How does language shape one's experience of neurodivergence?

In the context of English, the use of terms like 'deficiency' and 'disorder' have made it possible for neurodivergent people to be socially marginalised because of their assumed deficits. Our linguistic choices have informed our cultural understandings of neurodivergence and of disability, to the point that simply existing might cause one to be labelled a 'burden' on society. Discussing the consequences of linguistic practices in the context of autism research, one study even suggested that 'language seemed to act as a tool of normalization of violence', allowing ableist attitudes towards autistic people to become commonplace.[2]

If we understand language as a historical and material force that shapes our reality, then language itself can be understood as impacting both the neurodivergent experience and the very idea of neurodivergence. When you hear the language used to describe neurodivergence, what does it mean to you? What language would help expand our practices against neuronormativity?

Language is a tool through which we can create our world and control what it is like to exist within it as a neurodivergent person. If 'our words make worlds', then we have the power to ask: What should we build next?[3]

A Crisis of Care

The privatisation of care does not benefit anyone. Privatising care, both monetarily and in the suggestion that it must be undertaken in private settings – for example, only within the nuclear family – allows it to be commodified, withheld, and used to impose ideas of morality upon the wider population. (Who is 'worthy' of the care they request? What should be considered vital care?) Neoliberal notions of wellness and self-improvement have also forced us into believing that care should be an individualised matter, dealt with through the spending of endless sums of money on anything that offers the prospect of self-enhancement.

Viewing care in this way has led to the destruction of social welfare and community-based practices. In the UK budgets for public services have been cut year after year, abandoning those who depend on them. This decision to put profits before people has led to what has been dubbed 'the crisis of care' – a situation that was only amplified during the chaos of the Covid-19 pandemic. As recently as September 2023, a BBC investigation found that the extent of these failures to care for neurodivergent people has led to the unnecessary deaths of dozens of young autistic people in the UK. Issues that were flagged ten years ago continue to be played out repeatedly.[4]

The idea of 'interdependence' can be understood as a

rejection of these decisions to prioritise individual resilience and focuses instead on ensuring that individuals are able to maintain a right to their autonomy, even if they depend on others on a day-to-day basis. It rejects the supposed 'shame' that our current society projects onto anyone in need of help and argues instead that we should be putting care for each other and our communities at the forefront of our lives.

A politics informed by neurodiversity and interdependence insists that our survival depends on the care of others, and that we all deserve to have our needs met through collectively owned forms of care, societal systems, and spaces. The Care Collective – a set of authors who came together in 2017 to understand the crises of care that we face – argues for 'promiscuous care', an indiscriminate form of care that flows to and from anyone who needs it and relies on more expansive ideals of kinship.

Its members write that 'to encourage promiscuous care means building institutions that are capricious and agile enough to recognise and resource wider forms of care at the level of kinship'.[5] Neurodiversity plays a role here in developing an understanding of how the needs of neurodivergent people might be factored into the construction of such institutions.

One advocate working to establish resources that will benefit the lives of many neurodivergent people is Jordyn Zimmerman. A non-speaking autistic person, she was appointed to the President's Committee for People with Intellectual Disabilities in 2022, and advocates for the use of alternative communication. As the board chair of CommunicationFIRST, Zimmerman says the organisation's mission is 'to protect and advance the rights, autonomy, opportunity and dignity of people with speech-related disabilities through public engagement, policy and practice reform and systemic advocacy'.[6]

Understanding access to communication for disabled people as a human right, Zimmerman exposes the ways in which not communicating through speech may lead to an ableist assumption that you have nothing to express or share, or that your communication is less valuable because it is not expressed through the most dominant medium. She fights for communication tools to be accessible, and for those with intellectual disabilities to be given more autonomy in their lives through the use of supported decision-making initiatives. Given the large number of autistic people who are non-speaking and/or have intellectual disabilities, this kind of work is crucial to the success of the neurodiversity campaign.

With a failing NHS in the UK and a privatised system that regularly refuses care to those unable to pay in the United States, health care itself is a pressing issue for many neurodivergent people. The experiences of neurodivergent people in these systems are often dictated by the dominance of the medical model. As I mentioned in Chapter 1, this model locates any disability associated with neurodivergence as an individual problem that must be diagnosed and 'cured'.

This view of neurodivergence as a form of pathology has informed much of the therapy and treatments discussed in previous chapters, such as Løvaas's infamous applied behaviour analysis (ABA). This led to the proliferation of therapies that aim to 'fix' what is considered broken in neurodivergent people, with ABA becoming the 'gold standard' for such treatments.

In more recent times, a tidal wave of efforts to discontinue therapies like ABA has arisen in direct response to the grow-ing neurodiversity campaign. As advocates seek to dispel the myth that autism is a disease, they argue that this means it does not require 'treatment', and that such therapies do not align with the understanding of neurodivergence as a regular form of cognitive functioning. This line of thinking has been backed by research suggesting not only that ABA exacerbates PTSD symptoms in its subjects, but also that it is fundamentally unethical, infringing upon the rights of both autistic people and their families.[7]

While a growing body of research shows that there is very little evidence that behavioural therapies like ABA are even effective, the parents of multiply marginalised autistic children may turn to ABA in increasing numbers when they feel they have no other choice.[8] This is the sense of 'hopelessness' that Løvaas preyed upon, and addressing that hopelessness should be one of our priorities if we hope to take neurodiversity seri-ously. If we want to argue that neurodivergent people have a right to exist freely without experiencing abuse or forced compliance, then we must create the space for them to do so safely. We must find ways to support both them and their families, to provide the day-to-day care that gives them the freedom to be themselves, and to ensure that parents do not burn themselves out by spending every day fiercely advocating for their children's rights. We must interrogate the forces that leave parents with no choice but to ask that their child suppress their behaviours in order to keep them alive and safe.

What would care look like when it no longer sought to eliminate neurodivergent people's autonomy, to insist that they are broken – when, in short, they were no longer being pressured to change?

It is undeniable that much of the care crisis outlined above is the result of capitalist systems that benefit the few and make life all but miserable for the many. Capitalism is obstructing our ability to relate and connect to one another, forcing us further apart, and leaving many to spend day after day simply trying to survive.

Material conditions for many neurodivergent people meanwhile continue to deteriorate. Capitalism views disability and the inability to work as moral failings and encourages us to turn on those we believe are being given 'a free ride'. Requiring care or material support therefore leaves you open to derision as you must confront accusations of personal inadequacy and the demand to prove yourself deserving of vital resources.

It is in this context that calls for interventions like universal basic income, degrowth economics, and wealth redistribution sound most promising. We have enough resources to ensure each person on the planet has enough to get by; but achieving this will require many to give up their visions of capitalist luxury. Neurodiversity will always be anti-capitalist.

A Greater Understanding

Knowledge is obviously indispensable for determining the type of treatment that neurodivergent people and their loved ones experience or require. Most people do not understand or have much experience with neurodivergence or disability. While the popularisation of the movement continues, most people still lack sufficient understanding of the topic, and often harbour outdated views, regardless of how good their intentions may be.

This is a symptom of a society that so often neglects disabled people, often viewing them as second-class citizens. If one does not have a direct connection to the experiences of neurodivergence and disability, one is unlikely to have much interest in understanding them, or listening to those who have experiences they want to share. Despite the fact that most people will encounter neurodivergent people in their workplaces, in their schools, and in their social circles, this lack of understanding can leave us socially marginalised or alienated. It puts us at risk.

As a possible solution, many have called for generalised training in neurodiversity and the creation of accessible environments, as well as early-years education on the topic – training and education designed and led by neurodivergent people themselves, which allow us to communicate our own experiences and trusts us to find our own solutions.

A greater understanding of neurodivergence, combined with its destigmatisation, may enable greater inclusion in communities and enhanced friendships and relationships – something many neurodivergent people long for. Supporting this inclusion may necessitate additional funding for groups such as MENCAP, which run social groups and activities specifically for neurodivergent individuals. This inclusion would require us, as Devon Price suggests, to broaden our social norms and reject the ideas of what is 'normal' that have plagued us for so long.

It is to be hoped that the more people gain an understanding of the way in which neurodivergence is currently penalised in our world, the more people will cultivate the compassion to demand something different. As neurodivergent people deisgn and build more neurodivergent-affirming practices and ways of doing things, these innovations can be shared and accepted, prompting broader change.

We can also hope that, by valuing the work of people like those mentioned in this book – those who are already invested in movements that work towards things like anti-racism, anti-imperialism, anti-capitalism, feminism, and queer and trans liberation – the value of combating neuronormativity alongside those movements will become clear.

The value of cross-movement solidarity, and the reasons why it makes sense to combat these forms of oppression simultaneously, is vividly apparent. The logic, for example, of ending practices that have their roots in eugenic discrimination against neurodivergent people will also be seen to clearly require an end to contemporary practices that target racial minorities, other disabled people, and the working class.

꙳

In order for the neurodiversity campaign to achieve anything significant, a greater understanding of neurodiversity must be accompanied by the destruction of ableist beliefs, practices, and systems. We must extinguish ableism at its root, eliminating it wherever it springs up. This will require diligence, and a commitment to having open, complex conversations about disability.

This will require non-disabled people to consider and notice the inaccessibility of much of our world, how commonplace non-disabled supremacy is, and the ways in which the medical-industrial complex formulates beliefs around 'good' bodies and minds versus 'bad' ones. It will require non-disabled people not to ignore things for the sake of their own convenience or brush off ableism and disability as a non-issue because their lives are not impacted by the violence and oppression they elicit.

It will require, as Mia Mingus notes, that we 'not only make sure things are accessible, but also work to transform the conditions that created that inaccessibility in the first place'.[9]

Looking to the Future

Over the years, many have bemoaned the state of autism research, and tensions between the autistic community and academic researchers have never been more pronounced. Research into autism has always focused heavily on the biology behind autism, as many have searched for (and failed to pinpoint) a genetic cause for autism. This effort, which hints at a desire to find and eliminate the cause, has accounted for the vast majority of research funding for many years.

As we can see in the case of Spectrum10K, the more autistic people organise to create change in this area, the more impact they may begin to have on the character of research. For perhaps the first time, those who conduct research into autistic people's lives are being held accountable for the consequences of their research, including the attitudes towards autistic people that it might cultivate.

Neither is research that focuses primarily on medical intervention into neurological conditions limited to autism. Work on 'CRISPR babies', to enable successful genome editing, continues in the hope of preventing the birth of children with Down syndrome.[10] Meanwhile, researchers in France reported in 2017 that, by studying the eyes of dyslexic people, they might have found the cause and a cure for the condition.[11]

When we trust neurodivergent people's accounts of their own lives and experiences, we can use this information to understand what more inclusive and useful research might look like. Instead of continuing the pursuit of possible causes and cures, we have the opportunity to ask what research would be most beneficial for neurodivergent people. Such research might focus, for example, on ways to improve quality of life for neurodivergent people, and how to deal with the current barriers to social inclusion they battle every day. It might look at the best ways to provide housing and stable employment, or to expand education so that it is more inclusive. It may capture the experiences of neurodivergent parents or consider what types of support are most needed by parents caring for neurodivergent people with high or fluctuating support needs.

In a recent post, MENCAP noted that those with learning disabilities have asked for resources and services that would help them to understand their emotional well-being.[12] By giving neurodivergent people the opportunity to discuss what they would find helpful, we can work towards offering what is most urgently needed – and find out what is currently missing, so that it can be developed.

In order to do work like this, which is participatory and centres neurodivergent people, we must offer them epistemic authority. In recent years, some researchers have argued that autistic people do not belong within the process of creating knowledge about autism. They suggest that being autistic bars them from being a credible source of information on their own experiences of autism.[13]

This speaks to the ableism that dominates so much of autism research and demonstrates the ways in which autistic people have been understood in some circles as being 'subhuman' – unable to offer any sort of expertise even in relation to their own lives.

In order to develop research that focuses properly on the priorities of neurodivergent people, we must combat such ableism, trusting that they can act as co-researchers and participants in the work that will no doubt go on to shape their lives through policy and public opinion. Any research that is done must be conducted in alignment with the views of neurodivergent people themselves, tackling the dehumanisation that has been rampant for so long, and taking into consideration the calls for change that the neurodiversity movement has advanced.

Political Potential

Any fight for liberation that does not include the plight of autistic people, neurodivergent people, disabled people, and all those whose lives inhabit any of those categories, is not a fight for liberation at all.

Neurodiversity constitutes an invaluable reservoir of thoughts, practices, beliefs, and perspectives that can be harnessed in the service of a better future. I don't believe that neurodivergence is a barrier to a 'good life'; I understand how so many of our socially and culturally constructed ideas of a good life are currently informed by capitalist ideas of productivity that can enable the alienation and marginalisation of neurodivergent people.

As Mariame Kaba asserts, 'hope is a discipline': it is an expansive practice that allows us to imagine, create, and build something new.[14] I believe, similarly, that hope is a choice we make every day: hope that our imaginations are broad enough to find alternative and novel ways of existing that we cannot yet begin to comprehend; hope for more joy.

In its commitment to offering agency to a group of people so often confined to a strict narrative that fails to account for their wants and needs, neurodiversity is thoroughly political.

It seeks to place neurodivergent people at the forefront of a conversation that has so often been *about* them rather than *with* them.

The political potential of neurodiversity is not to be forgotten. Rejecting neuronormativity is a political act.

There is room for us all.

Acknowledgements

Thank you first and foremost to all the people whose thinking, writing, organising, researching, working, caring, and collaborating has moved neurodiversity forward. Thank you for carving out a place in the world for ideas like these.

Thank you to every autistic person who has ever made me feel less alone.

Thank you to Leo Hollis. A kind and patient editor whose enthusiasm for this book has been a gift.

Thank you to my parents, family, and friends for your endless care and acceptance. Thank you for giving me breathing room when I need it. Thank you for letting me talk about the things that matter to me and thank you for listening even when you get bored.

And finally, thank you to Catherine and Elisa. This book exists in part thanks to your encouragement. Onwards and sidey-ways.

FURTHER READING/LISTENING

Books

Empire of Normality: Neurodiversity and Capitalism, Robert Chapman
A Day with No Words, Tiffany Hammond
Stim: An Autistic Anthology, edited by Lizzie Huxley-Jones
Unmasking Autism: The Power of Embracing Our Hidden Neurodiversity,
    Dr Devon Price
Neuroqueer Heresies, Nick Walker
We're Not Broken: Changing the Autism Conversation, Eric Garcia
*Untypical: How the World isn't Built for Autistic People and What We
    Can Do About It*, Pete Wharmby
Health Communism: A Surplus Manifesto, Artie Vierkant and Beatrice
    Adler-Bolton
Mad World: The Politics of Mental Health, Micha Frazer-Carroll
The Care Manifesto: The Politics of Interdependence, The Care Collective
Autism in Adulthood (journal), editor-in-chief, Christina Nicolaidis

Websites

Neuroclastic's Directory of Nonspeaker pages, blogs, & Media, neuroclastic.com.

Sin's Invalid, sinsinvalid.org

Project LETS, projectlets.org

'Autistic Experience in the Majority World', youtube.com

The Spiral Lab, youtube.com

The Centre for Research in Autism and Education, youtube.com

Neuromancers, neuromancersmagazine.com

Open Future Learning, openfuturelearning.org

Podcasts

Death Panel

Disorderland

Instagram:

@projectslets

@neuromancers_

@sinsinvalid

@neuroclastic

@nigh.functioning.autism

@fidgets.and.fries

@drdevonprice

@blackneurodiversity

@dandelion.hill

@nonspeakers.r.us

@open_future_learning

NOTES

Introduction

1 Throughout this book I will use identity-first language ('autistic person') rather than person-first language ('person with autism'). This is my preference and reflects that of the autistic people I know. It is worth noting that not all autistic people prefer this, and that is okay too. Many autistic people have written pieces online that explain their preference for identity-first language and why this language matters to them. But, to put it briefly, I would never call myself a 'person with lesbianism'. I am a lesbian: it is part of who I am.

2 'Neurodivergent' was coined by Kassiane Asasumasu.

3 Niko McCarty, 'Psychiatric Conditions Hospitalize Almost One in Four Autistic Women by Age 25', *Spectrum News*, 31 October 2022, at spectrumnews.org.

4 David Gray-Hammond, 'Autism, ADHD, Tourette's, Dyslexia: Higher Risk for Addiction & Suicide – #NoDejahVu', 9 September 2020, at neuroclastic.com.

5 Joseph Guan and Guohua Li, *Injury Mortality in Individuals with Autism*, 21 March 2017, at ajph.aphapublications.org.

6 Robert D. Austin and Gary P. Pisano, 'Neurodiversity Is a Competitive Advantage: Why You Should Embrace It in Your Workforce', *Harvard Business Review*, May–June 2017, at hbr.org.

7 Jonny Thompson, 'Does the Term "Neurodiversity" Do More Harm than Good?', *Big Think*, 12 July 2021, at bigthink.com.

8 Throughout this book I will refer to autism as a disability. Autism is considered a disability from both a medical and a legal standpoint, and many autistic people identify as disabled. Not all autistic people see their autism as a disability, and I do not seek to impose my usage. I will, however, ask that people interrogate their reluctance to use the word 'disabled'. Being disabled is not shameful, and I will not treat it as such.

9 Marta Rose, @divergent_design_studios on Instagram, 2021, at instagram.com.

10 David Graeber, *The Utopia of Rules: On Technology, Stupidity, and the Secret Joys of Bureaucracy* (New York: Melville House, 2016), p. 53.

11 Judy Singer, 'Odd People In: The Birth of Community Amongst People on the Autism Spectrum: A Personal Exploration of a New Social Movement based on Neurological Diversity', an honours thesis presented to the Faculty of Humanities and Social Science, the University of Technology, Sydney.

12 Martijn Dekker. 'A Correction on the Origin of the Term "Neurodiversity"', in Martijn "McDutchie" Dekker's blog, 2023, at inlv.org.

13 Jim Sinclair, 'Don't Mourn for Us', Autism Network International, 3 October 2012, p. 1, at philosophy.ucsc.edu.

14 Judy Singer, *NeuroDiversity: The Birth of an Idea* (Judy Singer, 2017), p. 32.

15 Judy Singer, 'Neurodiversity: Definition and Discussion', at neuro-diversity2.blogspot.com.

16 Mia Mingus, 'Changing the Framework: Disability Justice – How

Our Communities Can Move Beyond Access to Wholeness', 12 February 2011, at leavingevidence.wordpress.com.

1 The Neurodiversity Campaign Today

1 Judy Singer, '"Why Can't You Be Normal for Once in Your Life?" From a "Problem with No Name" to the Emergence of a New Category of Difference', in Mairian Corker and Sally French, eds, *Disability Discourse* (Buckingham: Open University Press, 1999), p. 64.

2 Judy Singer, *NeuroDiversity: The Birth of an Idea* (Judy Singer, 2017), p. 9.

3 Hannah Furfaro, 'New Evidence Ties Hans Asperger to Nazi Eugenics Program', *Spectrum News*, 19 April 2018, at spectrum news.org.

4 Throughout the book I will use 'learning disabilities' and 'intellectual disabilities' interchangeably, reflecting the language used across different regions.

5 *Disabled World*, 'Models of Disability: Types and Definitions', 10 September 2010, at disabled-world.com.

6 Nick Walker, 'Throw Away the Master's Tools: Liberating Ourselves from the Pathology Paradigm', 2013, at neuroqueer .com.

7 During the writing of this book, Singer shared a number of hateful views towards the transgender community and those involved with the neurodiversity movement, claiming that the current movement has become 'cultish'. These are views I do not share. While I have recognised and recorded here the contributions she made to the movement, I am greatly appreciative of those whose work takes us far beyond the limits of Singer's. There are many people working towards both trans and neurodivergent liberation, and

that is where I feel the greatest hope lies.

8 Given that I am not the sole voice of the autistic community, it is important to note that there are some autistic people who do not object to the use of these labels invoking levels of functioning, and we must allow for those experiences too. In these cases, people often find the terms useful for explaining what their life looks like on a day-to-day basis.

9 To read more about autistic joy, see Julia Bascom, *The Obsessive Joy of Autism* (London: Jessica Kingsley, 2015), and Jennifer White-Johnson, 'Autistic Joy as an Act of Resistance', 25 October 2019, at thinkingautismguide.com.

10 I use the term 'non-speaking' rather than 'non-verbal' because the work I have read from this group suggests this is their preferred term. If you are interested in reading work from more non-speakers, I recommend the non-speaker archive from *Neuroclastic*, at neuro clastic.com.

11 It is also worth noting here that, as of 2013, Asperger syndrome had been removed from the Diagnostic and Statistical Manual of Mental Disorders. This was a controversial decision but was decided upon in response to a growing understanding of autism as a disability that reaches far beyond a straight-line spectrum from 'good autistics' at one end to 'not so good autistics' at the other.

12 See Steven K. Kapp, 'Profound Concerns about "Profound Autism": Dangers of Severity Scales and Functioning Labels for Support Needs', 19 January 2023, at mdpi.com.

13 Heini Natri et al., 'Anti-Ableist Language Is Fully Compatible with High-Quality Autism Research' – a response to Singer et al., 2023, psyarxiv.com.

14 Ibid.

15 Mary Doherty, 'Weaponized Heterogeneity Only Harms the Most Vulnerable Autistic People', *Spectrum*, 17 April 2023, at spectrum news.org.

16 Singer, *NeuroDiversity*, pp. 42–3.

17 Patrick Dwyer, 'The Neurodiversity Approach(es): What Are They and What Do They Mean for Researchers?', *Human Development* 66: 2 (May 2022), p. 75.

18 Note that 'normalising' is understood here to mean that the goal is not to push a disabled or neurodivergent person towards 'normal' standards of personhood – for example, to become non-disabled.

19 Ashley Blanchard, Stanford Chihuri, Carolyn G. DiGuiseppi, and Guohua Li, 'Risk of Self-harm in Children and Adults with Autism Spectrum Disorder', *JAMA Network Open* 4: 20 (19 October 2021), at ncbi.nlm.nih.gov.

20 Robert Chapman, 'Neurodiversity, Disability, Wellbeing', in Hanna Rosqvist, Nick Chown, and Anna Stenning, eds, *Neurodiversity Studies: A New Critical Paradigm* (London: Routledge, 2020), p. 66.

21 Ibid., p. 67.

22 Gavin R. Stewart et al., 'Traumatic Life Experiences and Post-Traumatic Stress Symptoms in Middle-Aged and Older Adults with and without Autistic Traits', *International Journal of Geriatric Psychiatry*, 23 December 2021, at onlinelibrary.wiley.com.

23 Monique Botha and Eilidh Cage, '"Autism Research Is in Crisis": A Mixed Method Study of Researchers' Constructions of Autistic People and Autism Research', *Frontiers in Psychology*, 24 November 2022, at frontiersin.org.

24 Ibid.

25 Lily Roberts, Mia Ives-Rublee and Rose Khattar, 'COVID-19 Likely Resulted in 1.2 Million More Disabled People by the End of 2021 – Workplaces and Policy Will Need to Adapt', *Center for American Progress*, 9 February 2022, at americanprogress.org.

26 World Health Organization, 'Disability', at who.int.

27 Health Foundation, '6 Out of 10 People Who Have Died from COVID-19 Are Disabled', 11 February 2021, at health.org.uk.

28 For further reading on this, see NCD, '2021 Progress Report: The Impact of COVID-19 on People with Disabilities', 29 October 2021, at ncd.gov; Shubo Zhang and Zhang Chen, 'China's Prevention Policy for People with Disabilities during the COVID-19 Epidemic', *Disability and Society*, 16 June 2021, at tandfonline.com.

29 Open Access Government, 'Report Finds COVID Patients with Learning Disabilities Given Blanket DNRs', 13 October 2021, at openaccessgoverment.com.

30 Public Health England, 'People with Learning Disabilities Had Higher Death Rate from COVID-19', press release, 12 November 2020, at gov.uk.

31 Stephen Powis et al., 'Do Not Attempt Cardiopulmonary Resuscitation (DNACPR) and People with a Learning Disability and or Autism', 4 March 2021, at england.nhs.uk.

32 Devon Price, 'Seeking an Autism Diagnosis? Here's Why You Might Want to Rethink That', 4 August 2022, at devonprice .medium.com.

33 Lenny Bernstein, 'People with Autism, Intellectual Disabilities Fight Bias in Transplants', *Washington Post*, 4 March 2017.

34 Michael Roppolo, 'They Say Their Children Are Being Denied Transplants Because of Their Disabilities: A New Federal Law May Help Change That', *CBS News*, 28 February 2022, at cbsnews.com.

35 Tess McClure, 'New Zealand Denies Entry to Autistic Daughter of Immigrant Couple', *Guardian*, 25 April 2022.

2 Neurodiversity Is a Political Issue

1 Renate Lindeman, 'A Moral Duty to Abort', *Huffpost*, 21 September 2017, at huffpost.com.

2 Quoted in Steve Jones, *The Language of Genes: Solving the Mysteries of Our Genetic Past, Present, and Future* (London: Flamingo, 2000), p. 19.

3 *NPR*, 'The Supreme Court Ruling that Led to 70,000 Forced Sterilizations', 7 March 2016, at NPR.org.

4 Jasmine E. Harris, 'Why Buck v. Bell Still Matters', 14 October 2020, at blog.petrieflom.law.harvard.edu.

5 To read more about the history of eugenics, visit eugenicsarchives .ca.

6 For more on this, see Linda Steele and Beth Goldblatt, 'The Human Rights of Women and Girls with Disabilities: Sterilization and Other Coercive Responses to Menstruation', in Chris Bobel et al., *The Palgrave Handbook of Critical Menstruation Studies* (London: Palgrave Macmillan, 2020).

7 Quoted in Alisa Opar, 'In Search of Truce in the Autism Wars', *Spectrum News*, 24 April 2019, at spectrumnews.org.

8 Jesse Meadows, 'You're Using the Word "Neurodiversity" Wrong', 12 August 2021, at jessemeadows.medium.com.

9 Nick Chown, 'Language Games Used to Construct Autism as Pathology', in Hanna Rosqvist, Nick Chown, and Anna Stenning, eds, *Neurodiversity Studies: A New Critical Paradigm* (London: Routledge, 2020), p. 35.

10 Micha uses the term 'Mad' to reflect the thinking and political organising that exist under this name, and she capitalises it to highlight the political nature of these categories.

11 Micha Frazer-Carroll, *Mad World: The Politics of Mental Health* (London: Pluto, 2023), p. 19.

12 Ibid.

13 *Catch 22*, 'Neurodiversity in the Criminal Justice System', 12 January 2022, at catch-22.org.uk.

14 John Lewis, 'Researchers Debunk Myths about Autism and Crime', *Otago Daily Times*, 5 February 2022, at odt.co.nz.

15 David M. Perry and Lawrence Carter-Long, 'The Ruderman White Paper on Media Coverage of Law Enforcement Use of Force and Disability', March 2016, at rudermanfoundation.org.

16 *BBC News*, 'Elijah McClain: "No Legal Basis" for Detention that Led to Death', 22 February 2021, at bbc.co.uk.

17 Laura Crane, Katie L. Maras, Tamsyn Hawken, Sue Mulcahy, and Amina Memon, 'Experiences of Autism Spectrum Disorder and Policing in England and Wales: Surveying Police and the Autism Community', *Journal of Autism and Development Disorders* 46: 6 (June 2016), at link.springer.com.

18 Yvonne Roberts, 'Trauma of Autistic Boy Shackled by Police', *Guardian*, 16 February 2013.

19 Robert Chapman, 'Is Police Abolition a Neurodiversity Issue, Too?', *Psychology Today*, 2 July 2020, at psychologytoday.com.

20 INCITE!, 'Critical Resistance Statement: Statement on Gender Violence and the Prison-Industrial Complex', 2001, at incite national.org. INCITE! Women of Color Against Violence is now known as INCITE! Women, Gender Non-Conforming, and Trans People of Color Against Violence.

21 Joseph Shapiro, 'The Sexual Assault Epidemic No One Talks About', *NPR*, 8 January 2018, at npr.org.

22 NHS, 'Learning Disability Services Monthly Statistics, 2021', at digital.nhs.uk.

23 Jayne McCubbin and Ruth Clegg, '100 People Held More than 20 Years in "Institutions"', *BBC News*, 24 November 2021, at bbc.co.uk.

24 Robert Booth, 'Family of Autistic Man Plan Legal Challenge Over Care Conditions', *Guardian*, 2 January 2022.

25 Wikipedia, *Silent Minority*, at en.wikipedia.org.

26 Amelia Hill, 'Winterbourne View Care Home Staff Jailed for Abusing Residents', *Guardian*, 26 October 2012.

27 Robert Booth, 'Care Home in Kent Gives Families 10 Hours' Notice of Closure', *Guardian*, 6 December 2021.

28　Quoted in Kylie Cheung, 'Ruth Wilson Gilmore Says Freedom Is a Physical Place – But Can We Find It?', *Jezebel*, 21 June 2022, at jezebel.com.

29　Damian Milton, 'On the Ontological Status of Autism: The "Double Empathy Problem"', *Disability & Society* 26: 6 (2012), at kar.kent.ac.uk.

30　Noah J. Sasson et al., 'Neurotypical Peers Are Less Willing to Interact with Those with Autism Based on Thin Slice Judgments', *Nature Scientific Reports* 7 (1 February 2017), at ncbi.nlm.nih.gov; Catherine J. Crompton et al., 'Autistic Peer-to-Peer Information Transfer Is Highly Effective', *Autism* 24: 7 (October 2020), at journals.sagepub.com.

31　Mari J. Matsuda, 'Beside My Sister, Facing the Enemy: Legal Theory Out of Coalition', *Stanford Law Review* 43: 6 (July 1991), pp. 1183–92.

32　Licia Carlson, 'Cognitive Ableism and Disability Studies: Feminist Reflections on the History of Mental Retardation', *Hypatia* 16: 4, Autumn 2021, pp. 124–46. This article is from 2001 and uses language that is now considered outdated. For that reason, I will use more appropriate language to summarise the arguments it makes.

33　Robert McCrossin, 'Finding the True Number of Females with Autism Spectrum Disorder by Estimating the Biases in Initial Recognition and Clinical Diagnosis', *Children* 9: 2 (17 February 2022).

34　Casey Rentz, 'Black and Latino Children Are Often Overlooked When It Comes to Autism', *NPR*, 19 March 2018, at npr.org.

35　Licia Carlson, 'Cognitive Ableism and Disability Studies: Feminist Reflections on the History of Mental Retardation', *Hypatia*, 9 January 2009, p. 129.

36　Ibid., p. 131.

3 Neurodiversity and Disability Justice

1 Amanda Morris, 'Court Overturns FDA Ban on School's Electric Shock Devices', *New York Times*, 15 July 2021.

2 Ole Ivar Lovaas et al., 'A Behavior Modification Approach to the Treatment of Autistic Children', *Journal of Autism and Developmental Disorders* 4: 2 (March 1974), p. 118.

3 UK Parliament, 'Draft Mental Health Bill 2022', at publications .parliament.uk.

4 Elizabeth Devita-Raeburn, 'The Controversy Over Autism's Most Common Therapy', *Transmitter*, 10 August 2016, at spectrumnews. org.

5 Margaret F. Gibson and Patty Douglas, 'Disturbing Behaviours: Ole Ivar Lovaas and the Queer History of Autism Science', in *Catalyst: Feminism, Theory, Technoscience* 4: 2 (2018), p. 5.

6 Ibid., p. 9.

7 Ibid., p. 10.

8 Ole Ivar Lovaas, 'Behavioural Treatment and Normal Educational and Intellectual Functioning in Young Autistic Children', *Star Academy*, 27 September 1987, p. 8. My emphasis.

9 Brandy Zadrozny, 'Parents Are Poisoning Their Children with Bleach to "Cure" Autism: These Moms Are Trying to Stop It', *NBC News*, 21 May 2019, at nbcnews.com.

10 @auttobe on TikTok.

11 Tabika D. Brown, 'Look Who's Talking Detox Guide', at auttobe .com.

12 Lisa Sweetingham, 'Exorcist's Brother Says God Claimed Autistic Boy's Life, Not Defendant', *CNN*, 9 July 2004, at edition .cnn.com.

13 Miltinnie Yih, 'God's Role in My Son's Autism', Voice: Dallas Theological Seminary, 3 July 2013, at voice.dts.edu.

14 Jim Sinclair, 'Don't Mourn for Us', Autism Network International, 3 October 2012, p. 1, at philosophy.ucsc.edu.

15 For an example of a call for change, see Angel L. Miles, Akemi Nishida, and Anjali J. Forber-Pratt, 'An Open Letter to White Disability Studies and Ableist Institutions of Higher Education', *Disability Studies Quarterly* 37: 3 (summer 2017).

16 Patty Berne, 'Disability Justice – A Working Draft', in Sins Invalid, *Skin, Tooth, and Bone: The Basis of Our Movement Is Our People: A Disability Justice Primer* (Sins Invalid, 2016), p. 12.

17 'Disability Rights, Studies and Justice: Disability Justice', 2022, at resourceguides.hampshire.edu.

18 Patty Berne and the Sins Invalid family, '10 Principles of Disability Justice', in *Skin, Tooth, and Bone*, p. 16.

19 Mia Mingus, 'How Our Communities Can Move Beyond Access to Wholeness', 12 February 2011, at leavingevidence.wordpress .com.

20 Eve L. Ewing, 'Mariame Kaba: Everything Worthwhile Is Done with Other People', *Adi Magazine*, fall 2019, at adimagazine .com.

21 To read more about the lives of autistic people of colour, see Lydia X. Z. Brown, E. Ashkenazy, and Morénike Giwa Onaiwu, eds, *All the Weight of Our Dreams: On Living Racialized Autism* (London: DragonBee, 2017).

22 Read the full essay, 'We Can't Address Disability Without Addressing Race', at learnplaythrive.com.

23 Daniel J. Losen, Paul Martinez, and Grace Hae Rim Shin, 'Disabling Inequity: The Urgent Need for Race-Conscious Resource Remedies', Civil Rights Project, 23 March 2021, at civilrightsproject. ucla.edu.

24 Marti Hause and Ari Melber, 'Half of People Killed by Police Have a Disability: Report', *NBC News*, 15 March 2016, at nbcnews.com; Erin J. McCauley, 'The Cumulative Probability of Arrest by 28

Years in the United States by Disability Status, Race/Ethnicity, and Gender', *American Journal of Public Health* 107: 12 (December 2017), pp. 1977–81.

25 Theresa Vargas, 'Remember Neli Latson, the Black Teen with Autism Who Seemed "Suspicious" Sitting Outside a Library? Ten Years after His Arrest, He Still Isn't Fully Free', *Washington Post*, 10 June 2020.

26 University of Cambridge, 'Transgender and Gender-Diverse Individuals Are More Likely to Be Autistic and Report Higher Autistic Traits', 7 August 2020, at cam.ac.uk. See also Anna I. R. van der Miesen, Hannah Hurley, Anneloes M. Bal, and Annelou L. C. de Vries, 'Prevalence of the Wish to Be of the Opposite Gender in Adolescents and Adults with Autism Spectrum Disorder', *Archives of Sexual Behaviour* 47: 8 (November 2018).

27 See Elizabeth Weir, Carrie Allison and Simon Baron-Cohen, 'The Sexual Health, Orientation, and Activity of Autistic Adolescents and Adults', *Autism Research* 14: 11 (November 2021).

28 I am using 'queer' here to signify anything other than cisgender and/or heterosexual.

29 'Two-spirit' (2S) is a term used by some Indigenous people.

30 'Hospitals; the treatment of gender dysphoria in minors performed in hospitals and other licensed healthcare facilities; prohibit certain surgical procedures', at legiscan.com.

31 If you want to read more about neurodivergence and trans identity, see J. Logan Smilges, 'Neurotrans: Thorazine, HIV, and Marsha P.', *Transgender Studies Quarterly* 9: 4 (1 November 2022).

32 Shahar Shapria and Leeat Granek, 'Negotiating Psychiatric Cisgenderism–Ableism in the Transgender–Autism Nexus', *Feminism and Psychology* 29: 4 (10 June 2019), p. 503. My emphasis.

33 See 'Neuroqueer: An Introduction', in Nick Walker, *Neuroqueer Heresies: Notes on the Neurodiversity Paradigm, Autistic Empowerment,*

and Postnormal Possibilities (Fort Worth, TX: Autonomous Press, 2021), p. 160.

34 Ibid., p. 172.

35 Noel Titheradge, 'Children Punched and Hit Over the Head in Care Homes Rated "Good"', *BBC News*, 24 January 2023, at bbc. co.uk.

36 Robert Chapman and Havi Carel, 'Neurodiversity, Epistemic Injustice, and the Good Human Life', *Journal of Social Philosophy* 53: 4 (1 March 2022), p. 615.

37 Ibid.

4 Neurodiversity, Work, and Poverty

1 James Cusack, 'Autistic People Still Face the Highest Rates of Unemployment of All Disabled Groups', *Autistica*, 18 February 2021, at autistica.org.uk; 'MENCAP Employment – Research and Statistics', at mencap.org.uk.

2 *Epic*, '1 in 70 Australians Has Autism, and Only 40% Are Employed', 2 April 2019, at epicassist.org.

3 Editor, 'China Focus: Chinese Families Strive to Improve Lives of Children with Autism', *Xinhuanet*, 2 April 2021, at xinhuanet.com.

4 Amelia Horgan, *Lost in Work: Escaping Capitalism* (London: Pluto, 2021), p. 11.

5 Branden Khong, 'The Lifetime Costs of Attention Deficit Hyperactivity Disorder (ADHD)', Centre for Mental Health, 2014, p. 16, at centreformentalhealth.org.uk.

6 Scope, 'Disability Price Tag', at scope.org.uk.

7 New Policy Institute, 'Disability and Poverty', August 2016, at npi.org.uk.

8 Mónica Pinilla-Roncancio et al., 'Multidimensional Poverty and Disability: A Case Control Study in India, Cameroon, and Guatemala',

SSM Population Health, May 2020, at researchonline.lshtm.ac.uk.

9   National Autistic Society, 'The Autism Employment Gap', 2016, base-uk.org.

10 A 2021 study found that autistic people in the UK spent a lot of time considering whether disclosing their diagnosis would provide enough benefits to outweigh the costs. See Anna Melissa Romualdez, Brett Heasman, Zachary Walker, Jade Davies, and Anna Remington, '"People Might Understand Me Better": Diagnostic Disclosure Experiences of Autistic Individuals in the Workplace', *Autism in Adulthood* 3: 2 (7 June 2021).

11 British Museum, 'Sensory Map', at britishmuseum.org.

12 Helen Castle, 'Designing Buildings for Neurodiversity and Sensory Impact', *RIBA Journal*, 2 March 2022, at ribaj.com.

13 See stickmancommunications.co.uk.

14 Ravi Malhotra and Jacqueline Moizer, 'Crip Time, Castoriadis, and Disability Rights in the Workplace', 2023, at youtube.com.

15 Julia Espelöer, Julia Proft, Christine M. Falter-Wagner, and Kai Vogeley, 'Alarmingly Large Unemployment Gap Despite of Above-Average Education in Adults with ASD without Intellectual Disability in Germany: A Cross-Sectional Study', *European Archives of Psychiatry and Clinical Neuroscience* 273: 3 (May 2022).

16 Robert Chapman, 'Neoliberal, Marxist, and Intersectional Justice Approaches to Neurodiversity', *Critical Neurodiversity*, 31 December 2021, at criticalneurodiversity.com.

17 Horgan, *Lost in Work*, p. 13.

18 @Telegraph on Twitter, 2023, at shorturl.at/ablI6.

19 Frances Ryan, *Crippled: Austerity and the Demonization of Disabled People* (London: Verso, 2020), p. 3.

20 Disability Rights UK, 'Disability Benefit Spending Reduced by £5 Billion Over the Last Decade', 23 September 2018, at disabilityrightsuk.org; Jon Vale, 'Majority of Disability Benefits Claimants

Being Left with Not Enough to Live On, Campaigners Warn', *Independent*, 18 January 2018.

21   Social Security Administration, 'Facts', at ssa.gov.

22   Connor Boyd, 'Wheelchair-Bound Benefits Cheat Is Caught Falsely Claiming £17,000 in Disability Benefit by Photograph of Her Riding an ELEPHANT', *Daily Mail*, 22 August 2019.

23   Disabled People Against Cuts, 'The UN Report into UK Government Maltreatment of Disabled People Has Been Published', 7 November 2016, at dpac.uk.net.

24   For an in-depth discussion of the impact of government cuts on disabled people in the UK, see Ryan, *Crippled*.

25   Frank Mc Besag, 'Epilepsy in Patients with Autism: Links, Risks and Treatment Challenges', *Neuropsychiatric Disease and Treatment*, 18 December 2017.

26   See shapingourlives.org.uk.

27   Elissa Ball, 'Almost One-Third of Autistic Children in the United States Live in Poverty', *Spectrum*, 19 August 2020, at spectrum news.org.

28   CarersUK, 'Breaks or Breakdown', Carers Week 2021 Report, 2021, at carersuk.org.

29   House of Commons Library, 'Adult Social Care Funding (England)', at commonslibrary.parliament.uk.

30   Lauren Nicolle, 'Just One in Seven Secondary School Teachers Have Received Autism Training', *Learning Disability Today*, 1 June 2023, at learningdisabilitytoday.co.uk.

31   Office for National Statistics, 'Outcomes for Disabled People in the UK: 2021', at ons.gov.uk.

32   For more on this, see Patrick Dwyer et al., 'Building Neurodiversity-Inclusive Postsecondary Campuses: Recommendations for Leaders in Higher Education', *Autism in Adulthood* 5: 1 (13 March 2023).

5 Moving Forward

1   Yulin Cheng et al., 'Neurodiversity and Community-Led Rights-Based Movements: Barriers and Opportunities for Global Research Partnerships', *Autism* 27: 3 (April 2023).

2   Monique Botha and Eilidh Cage, ' "Autism Research Is in Crisis": A Mixed Method Study of Researchers' Constructions of Autistic People and Autism Research', *Frontiers in Psychology*, 24 November 2022, at frontiersin.org.

3   Language Acts and Worldmaking, 'Who We Are', at languageacts.org.

4   Ruth Clegg, Harriet Agerholm and Alison Benjamin, 'Young Autistic People Still Dying Despite Coroner Warnings Over Care', *BBC News*, 7 September 2023, at bbc.co.uk.

5   The Care Collective, *The Care Manifesto: The Politics of Interdependence* (London: Verso, 2020), p. 44.

6   Sara Luterman, 'Jordyn Zimmerman Is Redefining Communication as a Nonspeaking Advocate for Disability Rights', in *The 19th News*, 19 April 2023, at 19thnews.org.

7   Henny Kupferstein, 'Evidence of Increased PTSD Symptoms in Autistics Exposed to Applied Behavior Analysis', January 2018, at hennykdotcom.files.wordpress.com; Daniel A. Wilkenfield and Allison M. McCarthy, 'Ethical Concerns with Applied Behavior Analysis for Autism Spectrum "Disorder"', *Kennedy Institute of Ethics Journal* 30: 1 (2020).

8   B. Reichow, Kara Hume, Erin E. Barton and Brian A. Boyd, 'Early Intensive Behavioral Intervention (EIBI) for Increasing Functional Behaviors and Skills in Young Children with Autism Spectrum Disorders (ASD)', *Cochrane Database of Systemic Reviews*, 9 May 2018, at cochrane.org.

9   Mia Mingus, 'Disability Justice is Simply Another Term for Love', 13 October 2018, at leavingevidence.wordpress.com.

10　Heidi Ledford, 'Why CRISPR Babies Are Still Too Risky –
Embryo Studies Highlight Challenges', *Nature*, 10 March 2023.

11　Valerie Howes, 'Scientists May Have Found a Cause – and a Cure
– for Dyslexia', *Today's Parent*, 19 October 2017, todaysparent.com.

12　MENCAP, LinkedIn Post, September 2023, at linkedin.com.

13　Botha and Cage, '"Autism Research Is in Crisis"'.

14　Mariame Kaba, 'Hope Is a Discipline', *Toward Freedom*, 17
September 2020, at towardfreedom.org.